GROWIN' UP SKOOK

THOMAS M. MALAFARINA

Printed in the United States of America

FIRST EDITION

ISBN: 978-1-952352-25-6

Published by:

Crave Press

www.cravepress.com

For my beautiful wife, JoAnne.

Even though I dedicate all my books to you,

this one is more worthy of dedication than all

the others combined because it was your idea.

Thanks, Sweetie.

"It was very much like Norman Rockwell: small-town America. We walked to school or rode our bikes, stopped at the penny candy store on the way home from school, skated on the pond." - Dorothy Hamill

"There are things about growing up in a small town that you can't necessarily quantify." - Brandon Routh

"Living in a small town, one of the keys to survival was your imagination." - Nick Nolte

"When you live in a small town behind the Pine Curtain, you live inside your head a lot." - Joe R. Lansdale

"A small town is a place where there's no place to go where you shouldn't." - Burt Bacharach

"Being from a small town, no one else was going to breathe life into my ideas other than me, so I had to go out there and do it." - Matt Bellamy

"You have to get over being shy and just be comfortable with yourself, and I think that for me, if I'd stayed in a small town, I'd be a different person." - Marisa Miller

"I was born in a small town. And I can breathe in a small town. Gonna die in a small town. That's probably where they'll bury me." - John Mellencamp

"People never expected a boy from a small town to have a life like I did." - Kapil Dev

"I would never have traded my small-town childhood in Ashland, Pennsylvania, for anything. It is why I am who I am today." – Thomas M. Malafarina

"You can't go home again." – Thomas Wolfe

Chapter 1

As I recall, I awoke early that crisp June morning with my covers pulled up around my neck, feeling a chill that crept in during the night through my open bedroom window. It had only been raised a few inches, but in June in Schuylkill County, Pennsylvania, it can get mighty cool at night. I was nine years old on that Saturday in 1965, just a month or so from my tenth birthday on July 23rd.

Looking across at the other twin bed sharing the eleven-foot square bedroom space with me, I could see my younger brother George sound asleep, tightly cocooned in his nest of blankets. We had only gotten bunk beds recently, having shared a single bed for several years. George would be six on his next birthday, August 8th, and had just completed kindergarten.

I lay still for a few minutes, and instead of thinking about the fun I'd have with my friends over the summer, I was momentarily filled with uncertainty when I recalled the changes coming my way in the fall. I would be going into fifth grade, and that meant leaving the First Street School, where I had spent the past three years with kids from Ninth Street down to First Street and below, and heading up town to the W.C. Estler school building, the one we all called the Seventeenth Street School.

All my fellow "downtown" classmates and I would merge with the "uptown" kids who had been together in that building since kindergarten. We would be there for fifth and sixth grades. I hadn't been in that building since kindergarten, and my memories were that it seemed massive. I was now older, bigger, and more worldly at almost ten, yet the idea of being one of the new kids didn't sit well with me.

As I lay in the darkness of my bedroom, I reminded myself there was plenty of time to worry about school as we got closer to the end of summer. For now, I only needed to think about having fun. The school year was over, and a summer of great fun lay ahead. Even though it was Saturday morning, my first official day of summer vacation, my body was still operating on school time. So, at 6:00 in the morning, I found myself awake and ready to go; however, it appeared I was the only one in my family suffering from this affliction.

Looking out my bedroom window, I saw by the growing light that the sun was rising. I could see the Ashland High School, which sat behind our house. To the right of the school, I saw the tree-covered sloping hillside area we called The Pines. In the distance, although out of view, were the black silt-covered hills leading to the abandoned strip mine pits that separated Ashland from the town of Centralia.

I decided to go downstairs, get myself a bowl of Rice Krispies, and maybe watch a little TV with the volume down low until everybody else woke up. Nothing could beat Saturday morning cartoons, even if I had to sit close to hear them. At least with Mom and Dad sleeping, they wouldn't be able to yell at me for sitting too close to the screen. I'm pretty sure that I wasn't going to go blind or suffer radiation poisoning from the Philco black-and-white boob tube, or as my dad called it, "the idiot box."

Perhaps I'd bring the milk in from the insulated aluminum milk box on our front porch, where the milkman left it every few days. Fresh milk smothering my sugar-sprinkled Rice Krispies was a thing of beauty. But since I was alone with no one to supervise me, I could double the sugar I put on them. Ah, heaven in a bowl.

I crept down the hallway past the center bedroom my two older sisters shared. My sister Georgine, who we called "Jeanie," was four years older than me and had turned fourteen on June 8th. My oldest sister, Louiseanne, who we called "Weezie," would be eighteen on July 23rd. We were born on the same day but eight years apart. In fact, all of us Malafarina siblings were sequentially four years apart. I always joked with Weezie that I was the best birthday present she had ever gotten. Okay, maybe I wasn't joking.

Tiptoeing past my parents' bedroom to turn the corner and head down the stairs to the first floor, I heard my dad snoring and knew it might be a while until he and my mom awoke. It had been a long, tiring week for them, which was pretty much how every week went.

2

Dad commuted more than fifty miles one way to work, put in a full day, then drove home.

When I got to the living room, I walked across the floor in the dark to stand on the metal register grate as I had done every morning before school. It was how we heated our house. The warm air from the coal-fired furnace called a Heatrola in our cellar always came up through the register grate on the first floor, then up through the grate in the ceiling to the second floor, heating both floors of our house, although not very well. Every day, as we got ready for school, my brother and I would take turns standing on the metal register to stay warm as we got dressed.

But that morning, there was no heat coming up through the grate. Then I remembered it was June, school was over, and winter was over, which meant there was no fire in the furnace, and there wouldn't be one until school started again in the fall. It wasn't really that cold, and I was still wearing my winter pajamas, but I would have welcomed a little heat anyway.

It wasn't really that cold, and I was still wearing my winter pajamas, but I would have welcomed a little heat anyway.

I decided to go into the kitchen to make myself that bowl of cereal. But as I approached the kitchen doorway, I stopped, remembering the number one house rule: never go into the kitchen without turning on the light first. That might sound a bit odd, but growing up in Schuylkill County, Pennsylvania, in my hometown of Ashland, as I did, you learned to deal with and accept many things that I suspect people living in more civilized areas of the country never had the "privilege" of experiencing.

As I stood in the doorway between the living room and the kitchen with my feet firmly anchored to the floor, I stretched and reached around the corner, flipped the light switch, and turned on the overhead lights. The kitchen instantly became awash with bright lights, almost temporarily blinding me, but not so much that I didn't see the dozens of black, shiny, disgusting water bugs scrambling across the floor and scattering in all directions. They ran for cover under our metal base cabinets and other appliances, like the refrigerator and coal stove. These obnoxious bugs were ugly suckers, more than an inch long and a half inch wide.

Some of my friends who also had these unwanted guests in their houses called them cockroaches. That might have been what they actually were called. What did I know about such things? My mom chose to call them "water bugs." Maybe that was just her way of putting lipstick on a pig. I recall my mom telling me years later how my Aunt Rosie, who had moved to Florida, called them "palmetto beetles." Once again, that all sounded like a lot of turd polishing to me. A cockroach by any other name is just as revolting.

Whatever their correct name, these horrible things were big enough that we kids never wanted to inadvertently step on one barefoot and feel it squash beneath our feet. As far as I was aware, the creatures were harmless, but even the thought of warm bug guts squishing between my toes was something I didn't even want to imagine.

As I said, that sort of morning ritual might seem bizarre for some people, but for me, it was just another day "growin' up Skook."

4

Chapter 2

Growin' up, Skook? What in the world, you may ask, is a "Skook"? I think it would be prudent for me to get this all straightened out from the start. I mean, since the book is entitled *Growin' Up Skook*, it only makes sense that I explain it. If the word "Skook" sounds rather strange, that's likely because it is. In fact, to the best of my knowledge, it's not a real word; it's more of a nickname or a slang term.

According to the Urban Dictionary, the source for all things slang and vulgar, a Skook is a black-and-white tuxedo-colored cat. As interesting and informative as that might be, I can most definitely assure you that is not what this book is about. To the best of my knowledge, the word Skook, which I will define for you, has only been around for a few years, perhaps a decade or two.

Allow me to try to explain. My native, Schuylkill County, is located in the heart of Pennsylvania's hard coal region. In recent years, the county has acquired the moniker "The Skook." I have no idea when it started or who was responsible, but like many such nicknames, it seems to have stuck. In fact, many Schuylkill Countians have embraced the name.

So, if we follow a logical progression of things, if it's acceptable to refer to Schuylkill County as "The Skook," then it seems inevitable that those of us who are natives of The Skook would be called "Skooks." So, is it all coming together for you now?

You see, the reason for this nickname is that almost everyone, especially natives of the area, mispronounces the county's name. The correct pronunciation is "Skool-kill," but it's simply "Skook-ull" to most folks. The same thing is true for the Schuylkill Expressway in Philadelphia. Just about everyone I knew pronounced it "Skook-ull" Expressway, though, in all honesty, I've often heard people refer to it as the "Sure-kill" Expressway. If you've ever driven on it during rush hour, you'd understand where the name "Sure-kill" came from.

I'm a native Skook born in a "patch" called Big Mine Run, just outside of Ashland in 1955. A "patch" is a grouping of several homes, too few to be considered even a small town. My family moved to Ashland when I was about two years old. I grew up and lived in Ashland until I was twenty-four years old. So, I suppose that makes me a dyed-in-the-wool, coal-cracking Skook. If you're wondering if the name "Skook" bothers me or offends me, it doesn't, not in the least. I've been called much worse in my life because of where I grew up, so I suppose Skook is okay by me.

As a young adult, when I first started commuting to work in a manufacturing company fifty miles south in Berks County, I was often called a "coal cracker" by my coworkers. They meant it as an insult, but I wore it like a badge of honor. I was a computer numerical control (CNC) machine operator, then eventually a programmer for Rockwell International Corporation, and believe me, if you didn't have or evolve thick skin working with those Berks County shop boys, you wouldn't last long. You also had to be able to dish out the insults as well as take them.

So, as you can see, "coal cracker" didn't upset me. Later, since I was one of many who traveled south to work, I was also referred to as a member of the "coal region mafia." Some Berks County locals saw us as unwanted interlopers taking the jobs from Berks County boys. I never let the teasing bother me. I figured if they were busy calling me names, they'd be leaving somebody else alone. Plus, I had no trouble coming up with and hurling insults right back at them.

I was also referred to as a member of the "coal region mafia."

Schuylkill County is steeped in coal mining history. More than a century and a half ago, the area was abundant with jobs for those men daring or desperate enough to try to earn a living working long hours for little pay, risking their lives in tunnels miles beneath the ground digging anthracite coal, also known as "hard coal," from veins running through the earth.

These dangerous mining jobs attracted a special breed of immigrants, largely men from Europe seeking a better life in America. Mine workers came from Ireland, England, Germany, Scotland, Italy, Poland, and many others. The one thing those immigrants had in common was they were not afraid to work hard to build a better life for themselves and their families. They had strong family ties and a love for their religion and European heritage.

It was not uncommon to find clusters of people of a particular ethnic group living side by side, grateful for anything that might remind them of the countries they left behind. In many Schuylkill County towns, certain places were considered Irish streets, Italian

7

areas, or Polish neighborhoods. As a result of this melting pot of various nationalities and cultures, the dialect spoken in Schuylkill County is a mixture of bits and pieces from all those ethnic groups combined, and as a result, is quite unique. Some people call it "Coal Speak." I like to think of it as "Skook Speak."

I could write a chapter and probably an entire book on the nuances of Skook Speak. Maybe someday I will. For now, I'll give you one example and then scatter a few throughout my remaining stories. Below is a sentence in English followed by the Skook Speak version of the same sentence.

English: "I met several of my closest male acquaintances from Mount Carmel at the local Ashland Fire Company Social Hall, where we enjoyed several rounds of Yuengling Lagers."

Skook Speak: "Me and some lads from over dere in Marnt Carmal was hangin' at the Ashland Hosie, hoistin' a couple, two, tree a dem dere Ying-Yang loggers."

Native Skooks are also known for being friendly. When they encounter someone, they tend to strike up a conversation. It usually doesn't take more than a few spoken words for that person to ask, "You're not from around here, are you?" Part of the reason is they tend to be surprised by the outward expression of friendliness. The other is that anyone who has heard the coal region dialect can instantly peg you as a coal cracker.

I can vouch for Skook's friendliness, having relocated more than 45 years ago to Berks County and having worked for many years in Lancaster and York counties. Although there are plenty of friendly folks in these counties, most people tend to be a bit more reserved than Skooks are accustomed to. Or maybe Skooks are just a bit warmer than others are used to.

After being a Berks Countian for more than four decades, I have to admit that I have adapted, lost a lot of my Skook friendliness, and have become more reserved around new people I meet. Part of that is my natural tendency to be what I refer to as a functional introvert. And the rest may be that I have inadvertently found my comfort zone.

Regarding the Skook Speak mentioned earlier, I referenced dialects, as in plural. There is no specific or standard Skook dialect; there are many. Even going from one Skook town to another, some words are found to be town-specific and localized. For example, I grew up hearing telephone poles called "tellypoles." I always called them tellypoles and assumed everyone else did, too. Years later, I learned not only was "tellypole" a regional term, but it apparently was unique to Ashland.

If you were from the Hegins Valley, you would likely have some Pennsylvania Dutch phrases mixed in with your Skook Speak. If you were from Shenandoah, you might have many Polish accents added to your Skook Speak. By the way, depending upon where you were from in the Skook, Shenandoah might be pronounced Shendoe, Chendoe, Shanadoe, or Shenadoe, and I've even heard it pronounced Shanadoor. You gotta love Skook Speak.

When I mentioned the mispronunciation of the word Schuylkill earlier, it brought to mind a story from my youth. Back when I was in fifth or sixth grade, one of my elderly female teachers struggled fruitlessly to get our class to pronounce Schuylkill County correctly. This is not an easy task for a classroom full of kids who have heard nothing but Skook dialects their entire young lives. I recall the visible frustration on her face as, time and time again, she stood before the class, over-enunciating the word "Schuylkill."

She stood, slapping a twelve-inch ruler into her palm, perhaps making an unspoken threat. She stared at the room overflowing with young faces as if daring any of us to try her patience and feel the wrath of her mighty measuring device of death.

Taking a deep, preparatory breath and releasing a sigh, never missing a beat of the ruler-to-the-palm exhibition, she said, "Okay, kids, pay close attention; this is very important. The county you live in is not pronounced 'Skook-ull;' it is pronounced 'School-keel.' Repeat after me, children, 'School-keel.'"

Unfortunately, the only response she got in return was a rousing chorus of "Skook-ull." To the best of my recollection, not a single student was maimed or killed that day, but I have a vague memory of my teacher slumped over her desk weeping, and there might have been some gnashing of teeth. Then again, that might have been me remembering incorrectly or, more likely, the result of my embellishing just a bit.

She stood, slapping a twelve-inch ruler into her palm, perhaps making an unspoken threat. She stared at the room overflowing with young faces as if daring any of us to try her patience and feel the wrath of her mighty measuring device of death.

That was only one of the many grammar, spelling, and pronunciation faux pas I endured during my life, thanks to my growing up Skook. I suffered countless embarrassments because of my origins. Remember TV commercials for "Hooked on Phonics"? That system might work well for some, but not for kids growing up hearing nothing but coal region dialects.

I recall a time during one of my elementary school reading classes when I had to read a passage aloud. I read the word "cupboard" as "cup-board." My teacher told me I was pronouncing the word incorrectly. I asked her what the heck that cup-board thing was. She smiled knowingly and told me it was the place in our kitchen where my mother kept our dishes, plates, and cups, to which, in my confusion, I responded, "That ain't no cup-board; it's a cubbert." This is why, to this day, I am eternally grateful for spelling and grammar checking software and, of course, my editors.

So now you know what a Skook is and that your humble narrator was raised a Skook. As such, *Growin' Up Skook* is a collection of stories I have told my wife, kids, and grandkids over the years about what it was like growing up in the Schuylkill County town of Ashland during the 1960s and early '70s. Although most of these stories will focus on Ashland, it could just as easily have been any other small town during that time period.

Chapter 3

I think the best way to give you a taste of the Skook is to tell you a bit about Ashland, P.A. (For the record, just about everyone from Pennsylvania refers to the state as "P.A.")

The Ashland I recall wasn't much different from many other small coal region towns, at least for those kids fortunate enough to have been raised in a place that left them with so many fond memories. The town I'll describe to you no longer exists. I mean, Ashland still does exist, as do its current residents; however, the Ashland of the 1960s, the hometown of my childhood memories, no longer exists any more than the hometown of your childhood memories. Time marches on and brings many changes, some for good, some not so much. I suppose it's all a matter of perspective.

The 1960s were an extraordinary time in history for us all. The time is often described as the last decade of innocence before the so-called sexual revolution of the late 1960s. It was a time of unlocked doors, little league games, penny candy, block parties, neighbors helping neighbors, and childhoods spent outdoors and unsupervised from early morning until late evening. And it certainly did seem that our little world was overflowing with kids.

It was a time before bedroom communities and playdates, back when everyone in town knew everyone else, when milk was delivered to your door, and the idea of tamper-proof packaging was not even considered. We had a milkman who, every few days, would place a glass bottle of cold whole milk in the insulated metal mailbox on our front porch. I originally considered him a sort of milk Santa Claus, leaving my favorite drink. Later, I learned we had to pay for the milk, and the magical aspect of milk delivery was lost forever.

We had a milkman who, every few days, would place a glass bottle of cold whole milk in the insulated metal mailbox on our front porch. I originally considered him a sort of milk Santa Claus, leaving my favorite drink.

I was always one of those kids who was curious about many things but oblivious when it came to knowing what questions I should and maybe shouldn't ask. As a result, I often said things as they popped into my head, not realizing it might not be something I should say no matter how curious I might be. When I was in fourth or fifth grade studying science, my teacher explained all the distinguishing traits of a mammal: having live births, being warm-blooded, and several other factors, including the ability of females to generate milk to feed their young. My teacher explained that was how we got milk from cows. Initially, it all made sense to me.

Then she threw us a curveball. She said humans were mammals. I thought, "Wait a minute here! Hold your horses! Stop the presses!"

I went home for lunch, very confused by the scholarly events of the morning. I decided I had better get this whole human/mammal thing straightened out once and for all. I figured if I ran this by my mom, she would set things right and explain stuff to me. I rehashed the whole lecture for my mom, including all the traits mammals had, and my mom listened, nodding in agreement.

Then I said, "My teacher said we were mammals."
"That's right," Mom agreed.
I said, confused, "But if that's right, then that would mean you could give milk."
My mom stumbled for words for a bit, then said, "Well...um, yes...that's true too."
I said, "Then why the heck are we paying good money to have milk delivered?"

The ironic part of that story was I wasn't being a smart Alec. In my innocence and naivety, I was proposing what I thought to be a serious solution to help the family save money. As I recall, Mom wasn't pleased with my economic concerns but likely let it pass as just another bizarre idea from her creative but off-times weird son. It was also a different time back then, when kids were kept in the dark about many male/female things that kids seem to learn about at a much younger age today.

It was a time before personal computers, the internet, Big Brother, social media, not to mention pandemics and social distancing. It was also a time before all the technological marvels young people today take for granted and those of us of a particular age still find amazing and occasionally confounding. Don't feel bad. I've spent a lifetime working with computers and growing alongside them in the digital revolution, yet I still have problems with technological changes.

Many people will argue that back then, before the so-called technological revolution, it was a better time. But I'll tell you upfront: I'm not interested in participating in that particular debate. I will agree, however, it most certainly was a different time. Not a better time, not a worse time, just a different time. Today's kids would be no more comfortable in the 1960s than a child of the '60s would be if he suddenly found himself thrust into this decade. We all have many pleasant childhood memories of those days. I'm confident my children and my grandchildren have theirs as well.

I think the problem is that some of our memories may be accurate, while others might have been reshaped into a utopian vision, not even attainable in reruns of My Three Sons or Leave it To Beaver shows. In sharing my stories, I'll do my best to keep them as accurate as possible. So, in keeping with that idea, here are a few unembellished facts about my hometown.

Ashland was settled in 1850 and incorporated in 1857.

Ashland was named for former U.S. statesman Henry Clay's birthplace of Ashland, Kentucky. The current population of Ashland is a little over two thousand souls. When I was a kid in the 1960s, the population was more than double that number — over five thousand. The town was crawling with kids; baby boomers, they called us. We were everywhere and never had any problem finding another kid to hang out with.

It's a town made up primarily of wood-frame row houses with a smattering of brick and stone houses, which are mostly found along its main thoroughfare. These wooden houses are remnants of buildings once called "company houses." They originally housed immigrant workers from coal mines and coal breakers surrounding the area. Ashland is built on the slope of a hill that runs from its eastern lower end up to its upper-most western end.

Centre Street is the main street running through town, primarily coinciding with Pennsylvania State Route 61 which arrives at Ashland's southern end at Hoffman Boulevard. The first traffic light is located where Hoffman Boulevard intersects with Centre Street. At that point, Route 61 takes a ninety-degree left turn and then starts up the hill.

While sitting at that traffic light at Hoffman Boulevard waiting to make your left turn, you have a direct view of one of Ashland's most famous landmarks, the statue of American painter Whistler's mother, known as the Mothers' Memorial, shown below.

Centre Street and Route 61 travel up an incline together to what Ashlanders call "the toppa town," where Route 61 takes a sharp right and heads up another hill for a few miles to the infamous and now-defunct town of Centralia, which is a town with its own fascinating history. Centralia is best known for a mine fire burning beneath it for over 50 years. It still burns today. Centralia was rumored to be the inspiration for a horror movie called Silent Hill, although Centralia's story is neither frightening nor haunted, just sad.

I knew Centralia when it was a thriving community. I bought furniture for my first apartment in Centralia. During my two-year stint as a writer for the local newspaper, the *Evening Herald*, I covered many borough council meetings in Centralia. I remember the day a young boy almost died when a sinkhole opened up in his backyard, and he slipped down toward what turned out to be a smoking hole of smoldering coal.

If I recall the story correctly, it was his grabbing onto tree roots that saved his life. That incident was the beginning of the end for the borough. The government got involved shortly after that incident and discovered the mine fire burning beneath the town. It wasn't long after that the town started disappearing one house after another. Soon, it was all over but the shouting.

When I was a boy, my friends and I occasionally walked to Centralia, taking the scenic route, walking through the abandoned strip mines between Ashland and Centralia, using them as a shortcut. In case you were wondering, our parents had no idea we were doing this any more than they knew we occasionally would walk along the railroad tracks to Gordon and back.

These remnants of strip mining, these giant canyon-like scars cleaved into the earth, were also used as illegal dumps by some locals but were places of awe, wonder, and adventure for dozens of bored kids over the summer months. You could find anything from household garbage or broken appliances to complete automobiles at the bottom of these ravines. Hundreds of rats and dozens of feral cats also lived among the refuse.

If memory serves me, it was believed that a trash fire in one of these abandoned pits turned dumps might have been responsible for igniting a vein of coal which eventually led to the evacuation and destruction of Centralia. The coal still burns under the town, and only a handful of stubborn residents remain.

Ashland has another tourist attraction besides the statue of Whistler's Mother. This attraction was in operation for almost all of my childhood, at least the part I remember best. It's known as the

Pioneer Tunnel Coal Mine tour and the steam locomotive ride known as The Henry Clay, although residents all call it "The Lokie." It's located near the west end of town behind one of Ashland's parks, the Higher Ups Park, near "the toppa town." Whenever we heard the Lokie whistle echoing through town, we knew summer was on the way. There is also a state-run Pennsylvania Coal Museum in the same area, but that appeared years later after I was an adult.

Market Street and Walnut Street run parallel to Centre Street, as do several smaller streets, such as Arch Street and Brock Street. I grew up on Arch Street, where my little end-of-row former house still stands. There were two Catholic churches in town and at least four protestant churches. We also had a typical Schuylkill County phenomenon of having as many, if not more, bars and social halls as churches. Several medical doctors, dentists, eye doctors, and even a few lawyers called Ashland home. One of those doctors, Doctor Robert Spencer, gained national fame as an abortionist. I've dedicated a chapter to the good doctor a bit later since I have personal, although somewhat vague, memories of him.

We had a post office with a library located on a lower level behind it with a side entrance. There were two banks, the Citizens' National Bank and the Pennsylvania National Bank. Ashland had one movie theater called the Roxy, which was a second or third-run theater where I spent many hours watching classic horror movies. The Roxy had a balcony where couples went to make out. Two sets of seats were on each side of the balcony where someone had broken out the wooden arms that separated them. These were for heavy-duty, serious making out.

Ashland had multiple barbershops, a shoe repair shop, and a variety of restaurants and cafés. Danny Snyder's Boulevard Drive-In was on the south end of town just before you headed up the hill towards Fountain Springs. "Danny's" was the local teenager hang-out, and when bustling with young people, it bore a striking resemblance to a scene from the movie American Graffiti.

Down around Fourth and Centre Streets was Jake Sebastian's restaurant, and Wayman's restaurant was a few blocks west on the same side of the Street. In my opinion, Wayman's had the best fountain cherry Cokes and vanilla Cokes in town. Whenever we managed to scrounge some change, my friends and I would stop at Waymen's for a cherry or vanilla Coke.

I remember once when my friend, Eric, hadn't finished all his soda, leaving about an inch in the bottom of the glass. He added sugar, salt, and pepper to what remained and then stirred it with the straw. When I asked why he was doing that, he said, "If you leave soda, the waitresses will drink it. If they drink mine, they'll be in for a surprise." Eric was very bright and a good friend, but sometimes he said some really strange and often scary things.

Up the hill from Waymans, at Ninth and Centre, was the Marko Town House, formerly the Hotel Loper, whose restaurant everyone used for fine dining. It was a time when you got "dressed up"

to go out for dinner and could always expect the owner to stop by your table to see that you were satisfied with your meal.

The only negative about eating there was that North Ninth Street ran alongside the dining room, as did a sidewalk for pedestrians. Large windows were next to the tables along that side of the dining room, giving the patrons a prime view of people walking along the pavement and allowing the pedestrians to see you eating as well. By the way, "pavement" in Skook Speak is often pronounced "payment;" I have no idea why.

If you were a young man spending your hard-earned money trying to impress a girl, the last thing you needed was to have your classmates making faces at the window, pretending to vomit, or doing anything to screw up your date. Although this was a somewhat rare occurrence, one thing that was far too common was when a diner glanced out the window and saw someone sitting in their car in a line of traffic, waiting for the signal light to change, and, more often than not, picking their noses. On those rare occasions when I saved enough money to eat there, I always tried to get a table away from the Ninth Street windows.

Because of the expense, eating out was a luxury for many people, my family included. Most meals were prepared and eaten at home. This was before fast food and mini-mart gas stations with food prep areas. The Marko Town House also had a huge banquet hall upstairs where all our Cub Scout and Little League banquets were held. My maternal grandmother, Lucy Metzinger, was a waitress there for many years.

The Ashland School District, before it merged with Frackville and Ringtown to become the North Schuylkill School District, had multiple schools in town, most of which were condemned, either while I was still a student there or shortly afterward because of their wooden interior stair construction.

The Tenth Street School building is the only one still standing. It was purchased in the 1960s by a local contractor, brought up to code, and converted into apartments shortly after I completed first grade. It was located across the side street, a block from my maternal grandparents' apartment.

The First Street School building, where I attended second through fourth grades, was demolished some time ago and now is a parking lot, and the W.C. Estler building, also known as the Seventeenth Street School, where I attended kindergarten, then fifth and sixth grades, was torn down and is now the site of a Turkey Hill mini market.

When town students advanced to junior high school, we could no longer walk to school and traveled by bus to Butler Junior High School, just up the hill on Route 61, from Danny's Drive-in restaurant, which I mentioned earlier. That junior high school was once the senior high school from which my father graduated many years earlier.

The original Ashland High School building was located directly behind my house. Mine was one of the last few classes to graduate from that building. From tenth grade to senior year, I could walk out my back gate and be at school. That building was eventually demolished and is now the location of the Ashland post office. A new junior-senior high school was constructed between Ashland and Frackville in Fountain Springs.

One of the most significant differences between the Ashland of my youth and the Ashland of today was the number and variety of stores in the main "downtown" shopping area. Ashland was a great place to shop. It might not have been as impressive as the city of Pottsville at the time, but it did just fine for a small town. I recall several national "chain" stores such as Woolworths, the Army-Navy store, an A & P grocery store above the center of town, and an Acme grocery store near its far eastern side at "the bottoma' town." The Acme was initially located in a smaller building on Centre Street across the street and down from the A&P. Since Acme is no longer in business, the downtown building is now a Boyer's IGA (Independent Grocers Association) grocery store. Acme in Skook Speak is pronounced Ack-a-me. One of my father's favorite bad Dad jokes when I was little was: "The Ack-a-me doesn't have a bathroom, so you have to go to the 'A&Pee.'" In addition, there were other small stores not on Centre Street since almost every neighborhood had a penny candy store. As a paperboy who got to walk all over town, I never had a shortage of candy stores to spend my meager earnings.

Regarding stores for adults, we had Charles J. Daley's men's clothing store, Bracy's Pharmacy, Heinz Pharmacy, K and M Shoe Store, Gellert's dress store, Sebrecht's Clothing store, Raudenbush's Bakery, Workman's Supply, Roshoe's Jewelry, Shilling's Store with its soda fountain and pool room, Kitty and Dotty's Flower Shop, Ruth's Hat Shop, Leonard's Magazine store, and of course the Gay Store.

I feel the Gay Store needs a bit of explanation here. It was a local five-and-dime that existed long before the term "gay" was associated with any particular community of individuals. It was named for, I believe, the owner's daughter, who was named Gay. The business was actually called Gay Stores, plural, as the owner must have planned to have more than one location someday. However, everyone in town called it "The Gay Store." Some people gave the store owner the nickname "Hong Kong Harry" since many of his inexpensive items came from Asia. We kids didn't care where the stuff originated. All we knew was they were excellent and cheap. We loved the store. It was a haven for kids with only a little money to spend. In addition to a great candy counter, it had slingshots, pea shooters, six-inch tall plastic soldiers or monsters, cap guns, and rolls of caps, to name a few things. As kids of working-class parents, we needed to stretch what little we had, and the Gay Store was the perfect place to do just that. Back then, only "junk" quality items came from Asian countries.

In addition to the Centre Street store, Raudenbush's bakery also sold items on my Market Street paper route from their actual bakery location. On Saturday mornings, it was my job to go door-to-door collecting payment for the papers I delivered during the week. It's hard for me now to believe that as a thirteen-year-old kid, I could walk around town collecting money in a vinyl zipper bank bag and never worry about getting robbed. I might have $60 to $100 at any time in a white bag with the name and logo of Citizens National Bank boldly embossed in green letters on the outside, yet I was never concerned about getting robbed or thought anything of it. Maybe they really were more innocent times.

On collection Saturday, I often stopped at Raudenbush's Market Street bakery and bought a sugar-cinnamon donut. One of the workers was a man named John. I never knew his last name. He was the guy who would bring me my donut. If he wasn't around, when I walked in the side door, one of the workers would call for him by shouting, "Ho John!" When my brother George helped me with my paper route, we would laugh and say, "Let's go to Raudenbush's and get a donut from Ho-John."

When my brother George helped me with my paper route, we would laugh and say, "Let's go to Raudenbush's and get a donut from Ho-John."

Growing up in Ashland was a special time for me. It was at a time before malls started popping up and decimating the small-town shopping business model. Almost everything a kid could want was available in Ashland. So, if you indulge me, I'd like to take a moment

25

to jump onto my soapbox here; I want to point out that I find it ironic how the same shopping malls responsible for the destruction of small-town shopping are now being abandoned and destroyed all these years later.

The construction of what developers call "town centers" is even more ironic. These places are shopping areas built to look like idyllic small towns. Some even have residential apartments above the stores, although, in many such centers, their façades are as artificial as a Hollywood sound stage. So, bear with me for a moment while I sum up.

Over forty or fifty years, we've gone from small-town stores to shopping malls back to small-town-looking shopping centers. Not to worry, folks; I'm sure online resources like Amazon will eventually make short work of everything. Okay, it's time to climb down from my soapbox.

Back to the Skook. Growing up in town in the 1960s meant during the school year, you walked to school in all sorts of weather. (We had to walk two miles, uphill both ways, in three feet of snow, yadda yadda.) We would carry our books with their covers made from brown paper grocery bags to school, either in a hand-me-down bookbag or wrapped in an elastic rubber thingie with two metal clasps on both ends that you bought at Woolworths or the Gay Store. We didn't have backpacks back then, and even if they had become popular, most families wouldn't have been able to afford them.

You were assisted in crossing the street by a crossing guard known as a "patrol boy." He wasn't some retired old person with a stop sign but a fellow student wearing a bright yellow diagonal canvas band across his chest who teachers handpicked for that noblest, almost military-like position of authority. Even though the majority of Centre Street was also state Route 61, we never worried about the possibility of a patrol boy getting struck by a car and having his family sue the school district. I guess it wasn't something that happened back then.

He wasn't some retired old person with a stop sign but a fellow student wearing a bright yellow diagonal canvas band across his chest, who teachers hand-picked for that noblest, almost military-like position of authority.

Ashland was primarily a blue-collar, working-class town, and most families had four or more kids, so money was always tight. I had a few friends who were "only children." They were often the envy of the rest of us because their parents could afford to buy them things that larger families only saw on television (a black and white television, of course). I had two friends who were "onlies," Ronny and Eric, so whenever possible, I would look forward to an opportunity to play with their cool toys.

One toy that comes to mind is The Kenner Girder and Panel building set. The television commercials for these sets were awesome. Unfortunately, we couldn't afford such a luxury, but I did manage to save enough cereal box tops to get a small free set in the mail. When it finally arrived, I thought it was amazing. That was, until my friend, Ronny, got a huge set that dwarfed my humble, and to be honest, cheesy set. So, I never told my friends about my embarrassing tiny and free set and hid it from everyone. Instead, I hung out with Ronny and got to play with his huge collection.

27

Although to some readers, it might seem like I'm painting Ashland with a broad brush using idyllic paint, I assure you, I'm not. It wasn't Mayberry, North Carolina, and neither Andy, Opie, nor "Aint" Bea lived there. Ashland had its share of warts and darker underbelly, as all towns did, large or small.

When I was about seven or eight, I recall learning about some weirdo lurking around town and pulling unsuspecting kids, usually boys, into dark alleyways on their way to school. The guy was a child molester, but many small-town parents were completely unprepared for dealing with anything like this. Sex and sexual perversions were not something ever discussed between parents and children.

Because of the time, the social stigma, and naivety, working-class parents were ill-prepared to deal with a problem as seemingly insurmountable as explaining about sexual degenerates to their kids. Yet they knew they had to find a way to warn their kids to watch out for a predator like the one stalking the town.

My mom couldn't bring herself to tell me that the weirdo molested kids; that was a subject that I can honestly say never came up in dinner conversation. Instead, my mom tried a different approach with her seven-year-old supposedly innocent son. (She didn't know about our hidden stashes of National Geographic with bare-breasted native women.) She sat me down and said, "Tommy, you must be very careful walking to school. Stay clear of strangers."

To which I asked, "Why, Mommy?"

She reluctantly explained, "A bad man is in town, and he's pulling little kids into alleys and empty buildings."

I asked, "Why's he doin' that?"

Struggling to explain, my mom came up with something I suppose she thought might help and said,
"Well...um...he's...um...making the little boys look at dirty pictures."

To which I replied, "Wow! Cool! I hope he grabs me!"

I thought my poor mom was going to either faint or brain me. Instead, she took a different approach and told me the bad man would beat the boys up after showing them the pictures, and although this explanation was extremely inaccurate, it did keep me vigilant regarding strangers. Naked pictures or not, nobody wanted a grown man to beat him up. Years later, I got the real story from my classmates. I don't know what ever became of that guy or who all he might have molested, but I never did get to see any of his dirty pictures.

I mentioned earlier that Ashland, like most Schuylkill County towns, had as many bars and social halls as churches and, as a result, had more than its share of drunks. It had many World War II and Korean conflict veterans and eventually vets from the war in Vietnam and Southeast Asia.

We didn't have terms like "post-traumatic stress disorder" (PTSD) back then or any real help for suffering veterans. I grew up hearing the description "shell shocked." It was a blanket phrase used to explain why Johnny's dad was always drunk and maybe why Billy's dad slapped his mom around sometimes. Or why Timmy's dad couldn't hold down a job. Or why several families were dirt poor and "living on the dole."

It's true that my hometown, like all hometowns, had its share of blemishes, but it also was a great place to live and a great time to be a kid.

Chapter 4

We had an excellent group of friends in our small neighborhood and never had trouble finding someone to hang with. As I mentioned, most families had several kids, some my age, some younger, and some older. I'll do a quick rundown of some of the neighborhood kids.

In addition to my younger brother George and me, we had Ronny, Charlie, Dave, Bobby, Eddie, Eric, Davie, and Dale on the boy's side. The girls were Pat, Kris, Judy, Peggy, and Jan. Others occasionally showed up for neighborhood games, and some were from nearby neighborhoods. Also, most of us had older and younger siblings who were around sometimes, but the boys were the core of our group. We interacted with the girls, but when it came to climbing trees, building tree shacks, playing army, reading "skin books," calling each other names, grossing each other out, and telling scary stories, it always came down to some combination of boys.

Eric and Ronny were only children, and the rest had siblings. Eric was probably the smartest kid in the neighborhood, whereas Ronny was more athletic. They were both my age, as was Dave, who was quite athletic himself. Dave was Bobby's older brother, and Dave's older brother was Eddie. Charlie, Davie, Bobby, and Dale were a few years younger, closer to my brother's age.

As with all kids, our band of brothers had unique personalities. And like brothers, we often got tired of each other, argued, and then worked our misunderstandings out among ourselves. We never got our parents involved, and I suspect if we tried to, they would have told us to work it out ourselves anyway. That's just how things were done in the Skook. Your neighborhood friends and family were all you had, so you always found a way to work things out. My dad once told me when he was a kid, whenever he and his six brothers would fight, my Italian immigrant grandfather Pietro would tell them to "go downa da street anda fighta wit da Irish."

I hear many stories about younger kids nowadays complaining to their parents about something someone did or said, then the parents got involved, and before you know it, nobody is speaking to anybody. Growin' up Skook, you expected to be called names and ridiculed for any physical afflictions you might have. You didn't get upset or cry to your parents; you learned to handle it and come up with your own insults to hurl back at them.

If your ears stuck out, you were "Dumbo." If you had a long nose, you were "Pinocchio." If you had dirty feet, you might be labeled "fungus." It seemed the list of nicknames and insults was endless. Nowadays, it would be considered bullying, and perhaps that's what it was back then. The truth was, ragging on each other and calling each other names was our way of accepting each other. The only time we ever considered someone a bully was when some big kid threatened to beat us or made good on that threat.

We all knew who the town psychos were and did our best to avoid them at all costs. These maniacs were usually the biggest, strongest, and dumbest sub-humans in town. If you could talk fast and manage to either stay on their good side or keep your distance, you stood a good chance of surviving elementary school with all your appendages intact. The absolute last thing you ever wanted to do was make them notice you.

I became so skilled at operating below their psychopathic radar that most of these serial killers in training didn't even know I was alive. Another trick I mastered, which was risky and took a bit more intelligence and skillful manipulation, was to befriend a few of these knuckle-draggers. Once the word got out that you were accepted by one or more of these guys, the other crazies tended to leave you alone, especially if you befriended a seriously borderline insane type.

The key to making that trick work was to stay on the crazy guy's good side, which meant not saying anything to set him off. This was the tricky and dangerous part, as one slip of the tongue, one wrong word to one of these loonies, could result in an extremely negative outcome. You could literally go from friend to punching bag in a few seconds. This is where I developed a quick wit and sense of humor. Sometimes, the only thing separating you from a shower of fists was being able to think fast on your feet, deflect attention, and keep the psychopath laughing.

Sometimes, the only thing separating you from a shower of fists was being able to think fast on your feet, deflect attention, and keep the psychopath laughing.

We were typical kids of the sixties, spending our summers in a small Schuylkill County town, looking for fun things to do with what little we had to make those things happen. I often say that poverty is the fuel that powers creativity. Maybe we weren't living below the poverty line, but we certainly could see it from there.

Chapter 5

Unemployment was a normal way of life in my economically depressed county, and I suspect it still might be for many. The area was originally based on an economy that supported coal mining; however, when the demand for coal disappeared, so did the jobs, and the rest, as they say, was history.

Most 1960s mothers stayed home to raise their kids while fathers with barely a high school education did all they could to keep working. Many ambitious fathers like mine commuted fifty miles or more one way in carpools to work in the cities of Harrisburg, Allentown, Bethlehem, or Reading, getting up at four in the morning and not getting home until supper time. Others worked long-distance, out-of-town jobs, only returning home on the weekends. Some who learned a trade like carpentry, plumbing, or electrical services started small businesses, earning what they could locally. Still, others did whatever they had to do to survive.

When fathers were "laid off," they would collect unemployment compensation for as long as it would last, then do their best to find another job. Some dads often found "under the table" work for cash to help make ends meet. It seemed like everybody knew somebody who needed someone with minimal skills for a few hours a week for cash. It might be working as an unskilled laborer, house painter, roofer, cement mixer, or any other job requiring a strong back and the willingness to work hard. A lot of bartering also went on, where one type of service was traded for another.

Besides having my dad home to hang out with me, one of the things I enjoyed best about these slow times was taking advantage of government-provided cheese and canned meat available for those of us with lower incomes. In my opinion, this was some of the best cheese I had ever eaten. We called it surplus cheese because that's what was written on the box: Government Surplus. Nowadays, I'm told some people call it "gumment cheese."

In my opinion, this was some of the best cheese I had ever eaten.

One day, when I was about five years old, my dad was unemployed again, and he took me with him to pick up our surplus cheese. While we were waiting in line there, he met a friend who was also out of work. The man noticed me standing, holding my dad's hand. I guess he felt motivated to talk to me.

He bent down to be at my level and said, "So, Tommy, what do you want to be when you grow up?"

I don't think he expected the reply I gave him. I said, "Nutten, just like my dad."

My dad often told that story and laughed at the brutally honest innocence with which I had answered. But years later, looking back as a father, myself, I'm sure, innocent or not, it might have hurt him a little bit to hear his son think of him that way. It probably served to motivate him to work even harder. As the saying goes, out of the mouths of babes.

And work hard was what my father did for his entire life. There was nothing he wouldn't do to provide for his family. This resulted once in his being handcuffed by the Pennsylvania State Police to headboard in a fleabag hotel in the town of Bellefonte after discovering the load of goods he had been hauling might have been considered stolen. Dad had no idea this was the case, as he was just doing an under-the-table cash job to supplement his unemployment compensation. But in the perfect 20/20 vision provided by hindsight, he probably should have at least wondered about the load he was carrying since it was for a man known throughout Schuylkill County to have a questionable past.

I won't mention the man's name, but he was born in the late 1800s in Ashland and eventually was found beaten to death in his nearby Fountain Spring home in 1969. He was labeled a local "beer barron" during prohibition and had numerous run-ins with the law, including a shootout with state police at his home in 1939.

The version of the man I recall was a kindly old gentleman who owned a corner food store. His other illegal activities were not something little kids were concerned with. His colorful life story would certainly make for an interesting book for any nonfiction or true crime writer. Although on that fateful night in Bellefonte, my dad was detained, cuffed, and questioned by the state police, he was never arrested or charged. I believe that was his last moonlighting job for that individual.

Taking care of the family was always my dad's top priority and a lesson I learned first-hand by observation, and it is likely why I'm still working full-time at the ripe old age of sixty-eight as of this writing in 2023. As a young boy, I even had the opportunity to get hands-on experience in what it meant to go the extra mile for those you love.

One winter, when I was seven or eight and Dad was out of work, we must have run low on coal to heat our house, and he didn't have the money to buy more. You might wonder what you do in the dead of a Schuylkill County winter when you have no coal, money, or job. You do whatever you have to. You improvise.

My dad bundled me in my warmest clothes and long underwear and told me to get my wooden Flexible Flyer sled. I thought maybe we were going sledding, or as we called it, "sleigh riding." He told me we would do some work to help our family. I was excited at the prospect of acting like a man and helping.

Dad sat me on the sled with four empty burlap sacks, a shovel, and a pickax. He pulled the sled up Catawissa Road to an abandoned train overpass, where we found some trucks and digging equipment. Obviously, some bootleg strip mining was going on near the old bridge.

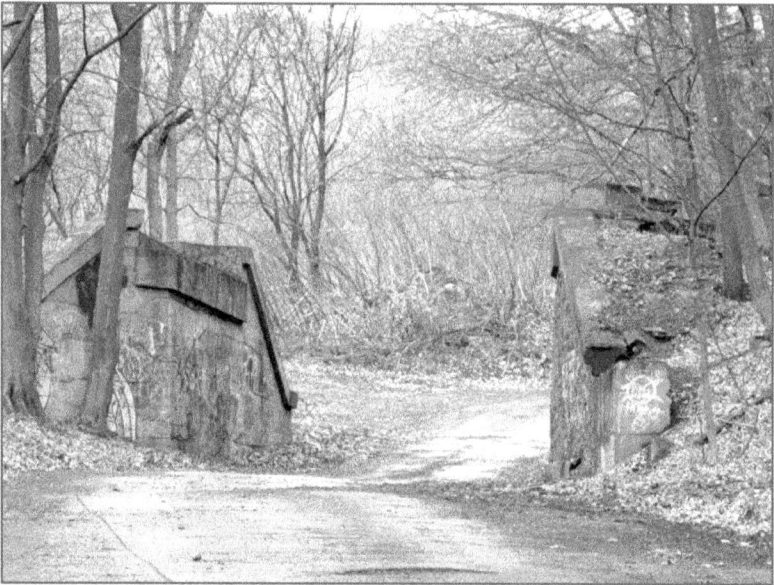

It was early evening, and the workers had gone home for the day. Even to an uninformed kid like me, it was apparent someone had been digging coal out of the ground and not necessarily doing so legally. Most of the real strip mines had been abandoned years earlier, but someone must have decided to take it upon themselves to see if they could find a few truckloads of remaining coal.

There was a lot of loose stuff lying around on the ground, not enough for the bucket on the equipment to scoop up, but plenty of scraps for scavengers like us. My dad quickly filled all the bags with coal, tied them shut with rope, and loaded them onto my sled. I walked alongside the sled as we headed home, ensuring none of the bags toppled over. This act, of course, was all wishful thinking on my part, amounting to nothing more than window dressing. Any one of the bags weighed more than I did soaking wet, and had they toppled over on me, I probably would have spent the rest of my life limping. But I felt like I was helping, and that's the lesson my dad wanted me to learn.

The next day, I got to help even more. I gained my official "coal cracker" badge of honor when my dad took me down to our cellar, and he emptied the bags on the floor of our coal bin. It was cold in there, so I was bundled in layers of clothing that allowed limited flexibility. Dad showed me how to separate the coal from the rock and break it into small pieces so we could burn it. He even let me put on a pair of safety goggles and an actual miner's helmet. I felt like a real coal miner, while through steamy, chilled breath, I proudly went to work.

You may wonder, did I stay there and break up all the coal in those four bags? I don't recall. I would like to say I did, but it was more than likely I didn't. I was just a little kid, after all. I probably broke up a small amount, then got distracted and did something else. My dad probably finished the job. But I recall how proud I felt doing my small part that would eventually help my mom, sisters, and baby brother. I felt like a man.

There was also a time when my dad got a second shift job in another town, maybe at Bethlehem Steel Corporation in Bethlehem, Pennsylvania; I'm not sure. I was only about six or seven. He used to drive my friends and me to school on cold mornings. One of his proudest memories of those times was when one of my friends, Kris, hugged him, and she told him he was "the bestest daddy in the world." It's always the little things that mean the most. My dad told that story many times and never without a look of utter pride on his face, one I will always recall and treasure.

These lean times spent with my dad taught me the importance of hard work and served as the foundation for building what would eventually become my work ethic, which I tried to pass on to my kids. In the world of low-income and tough economic times, unemployment must be constantly dealt with. Growin' up Skook taught me the importance of working hard, taking the bull by the horns, and controlling your destiny, regardless of economic conditions.

Chapter 6

Every small Schuylkill County town had an abundance of parks for kids. To my less-than-precise recollection, there were four or five parks in Ashland when I was a boy. There might have been more, possibly less. I'm a bit fuzzy on the exact number, as I only spent significant time at three of them.

When I say parks, I'm referring to places with shade trees, swings, slides, jungle gyms, and other things to help keep us kids from being bored during the long, hot summer months. Ashland did a great job catering to the needs of its many baby-boomer children.

These were much different places than the "tot lots" and "play areas" that decorate housing developments today. Everything was constructed of heavy wood and steel; there wasn't an ounce of kid-safe plastic anywhere. No six-inch thick bed of shredded tire mulch covered the ground to protect Junior's backside should he fall. These parks would be considered "death traps" by today's standards. But deadly or not, we kids loved them. Perhaps we were attracted to that dangerous aspect of these rides.

Some of the parks in town had been well maintained annually, with steel poles freshly scraped and painted every spring with a heavy coat of silver industrial-quality paint. Likewise, the thick, flat wooden swing seats were sanded and got a fresh coat of paint, and their chains could be seen glimmering in the summer sunlight with their own fresh coat of silver. I can't exactly recall the colors of the swings, but I believe bright red or forest green was often used.

The slides, which we called "sliding boards" back then, were of various sizes ranging from very small, about four feet high, to more than twenty feet off the ground. At least, that's what they seemed like to me. These wood and sheet metal monstrosities baked in the hot summer sun, waiting to assault the exposed legs of shorts-wearing youngsters.

Many kids burned their legs on those slides or fell and injured themselves, sometimes quite severely, and to my knowledge, no lawsuits were ever filed, and those casualties never even came close to discouraging any kid from using the equipment. If anything, it created a mystique that only served to challenge and attract more children.

Often, some kid would swipe a few sheets of waxed paper from his mom's kitchen and use it to turn the metal slide surface into a lightning-fast miracle of 1960s technology. It often only took a few trips down the slide for a determined kid sitting on the waxed paper to create an incredibly fast sliding experience. It was not uncommon on the larger slides to fly down so fast you would zoom off the bottom, sail past the deep dirt channel formed by thousands of sneakers, and into the grass where you would land on your backside, much to the amusement of your friends.

Our multi-story school buildings also had giant enclosed silo-like fire escapes attached to them. These huge cylinders contained circular slides inside. These two and three-story monstrosities were a thing of amazement for every kid in the school. We lived for "fire drill" day. That was when the teacher would pick a student, usually a larger, heavier kid, hand him a piece of wax paper, and let him prepare the slide for the fire drill. He usually got two or three trips down the tunnel of terror, whereas the rest of us only got one ride down the slide when the alarm bell rang.

I always found these drills much more enjoyable than the Cold War-inspired "drop and cover" drills. Even as a dumb kid with no knowledge of nuclear power whatsoever, I had watched enough World War II movies to realize that all I could hope to do by curling up under my desk during a nuclear confrontation was to kiss my butt goodbye. But at least the fire drills were awesome; it was like being in an amusement park during winter.

As I said, some of our parks were well-maintained, and others were rougher around the edges. Only a few parks remain today, while others have vanished into historical obscurity. Some of these parks also had baseball fields, serving as practice fields and sites for actual Little League games.

One of the older parks, which I always felt was not as well maintained as the others, was called Willow Park.

The park had swings, slides, and picnic pavilions. It had a baseball field where my farm teams played their baseball games. The term "farm team" refers to teams of children from around six to eight or nine years old. After that, you moved up into Little League until you were twelve. Once you hit thirteen, you had to play teener league and eventually high school league baseball.

I was particularly fond of the farm team because playing ball at that age was neither competitive nor serious. This was a good thing because no matter how hard I tried, I was probably the most pathetic baseball player to ever take the field. My dad was one of the coaches and did his best to try to make a ball player out of me, but to no avail.

Dad had quite the reputation as a coach. He carried a handful of small rocks, not much bigger than pebbles. Whenever he caught one of his players goofing off, not paying attention, or not doing what he was supposed to, Dad would throw a rock at the kid, usually just hitting him on the leg or foot. No severe injuries ever occurred, but plenty of stings and maybe a few welts did.

By the way, all the kids loved my dad and thought his rock-throwing was hilarious. It became something of an honor to be able to get hit by one of his projectiles. I can't even begin to imagine something like that happening today. I smell lawsuits and potential jail time.

What I remember most about the Willow Park of my youth were the trees. It was aptly named with what seemed like a canopy of willow trees blanketing the park in the shade and making a cool refuge from the hot summer sun. Even the sliding boards in Willow Park seemed less lethal than those at other parks with fewer shade trees. But even as a kid, I could tell Willow Park was old and had seen better days. The paint on its pavilions was often peeling and the equipment was worn, but I enjoyed it just as much as any wide-eyed kid my age would.

Another thing I remember was a ride, a multi-person swing consisting of two bench seats facing each other on a large, rectangular, heavy wooden platform. It hung suspended from a strong metal frame cemented into the ground and was usually a very relaxing ride. That was unless you made the mistake of getting on it with some of the town's more rambunctious delinquents and potential future death row inmates. (You know who you were.) At these times, the swing was pushed to and beyond its safety limits, leaving its occupants hanging on for dear life, imagining the bruises and broken bones that would follow if they fell from the ride.

On the southwestern side of town, known to residents as "the toppa town," Higher Up Park resides.

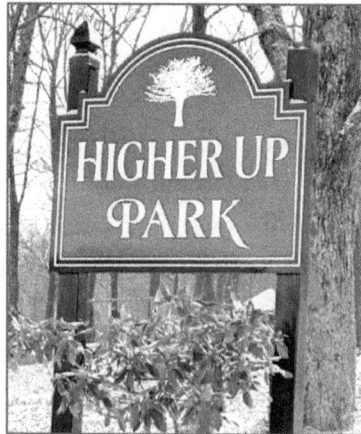

It was and still is the location of Ashland's famous tourist attraction, The Pioneer Tunnel coal mine tour and steam train ride. The train is known to residents as "The Lokie," as I mentioned earlier. Hearing its loud whistle all over town was a sure sign to us, kids, that spring had arrived, and summer was just around the corner.

The Pioneer Tunnel coal mine tour is a fascinating experience, and at a constant temperature of around 50 degrees all year long, the ride takes you down into the bowels of the earth, making a perfect escape from the summer heat. Unfortunately, as kids, we never had the money to tour the mine, so the most we did was just hang out in the shade of the trees, enjoying the swings, merry-go-rounds, and monkey bars.

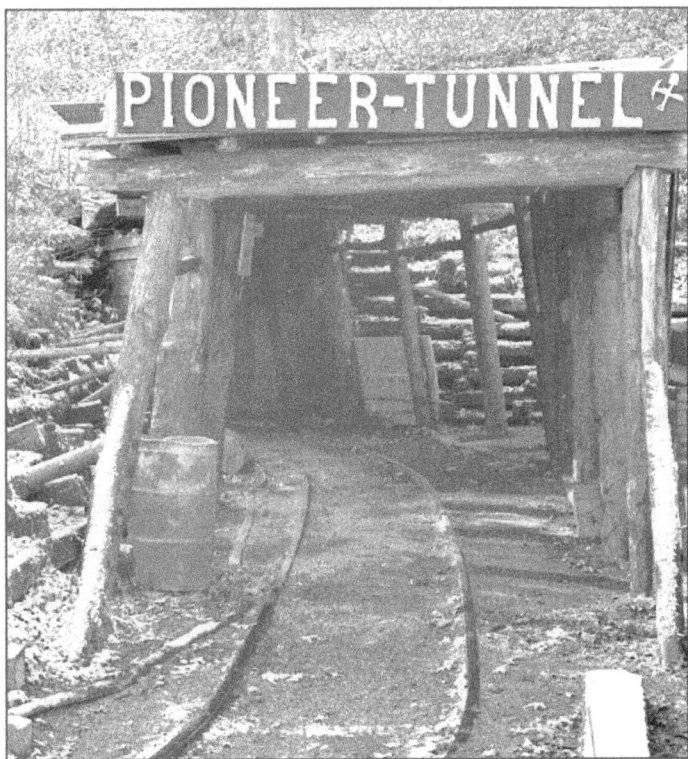

There were several pavilions in this park, and I recall our church had its covered-dish picnics in the one pictured below.

There was an awesome ride at the park when I was a kid, but now it resides in the Carousel Museum at Knobles Grove Amusement Park in Elysburg, Pennsylvania. For all of my youth, it was a ride we all enjoyed whenever we were at the Higher Up Park. It featured a large, majestic-looking painted lion suspended from metal rods and protected from the elements under a shingled roof in a small pavilion.

As a kid, I thought the lion ride was one of the most amazing things I had ever seen. I couldn't believe it was right there waiting for us to ride anytime we wanted to for free. Several of us would climb onto the lion's back and rock back and forth until it was time to give someone else a chance. Over the years, it began to show its age and the wear and tear it had endured. Now, it has been restored to perfection and can be seen by thousands of museum visitors.

Speaking of museums, the Higher Up Park area is also home to the Pennsylvania Coal Museum. It is a first-class state-run facility and is an interesting place with lots of coal mining history, photos, and memorabilia. It wasn't around when I was a kid; it arrived years later.

Across town from Higher Up Park is Eureka Park.

I spent most of my early teen years hanging out there. It was the main location for Little League baseball and had a great concession stand for inexpensive food and snacks. A cement bandstand was, and still is, located under some of the many shade trees, and I heard many of my favorite local bands perform there. They have since added sides and a roof to the bandstand, which is a great feature.

This was a high priority for a little kid learning to play guitar and dreaming about the day he could play on stage. I spent hours studying (not just watching) many different local performers in my youth, many of whom I eventually shared a stage with in later years.

Eureka Park also had one of the tallest slides in town — a double slide. A set of metal stairs zigzagged up to a platform high above the ground. From there, one slide went to the right and the other to the left. Whenever I look at old pictures of that slide now, I realize it was not so much something we enjoyed as something we were lucky to survive.

Another ride, the yo-yo, was also something you were lucky to get off of with all your limbs intact. The ride consisted of a long, varnished plank about two inches thick, a foot wide, and about twelve feet long. The plank was suspended from four metal poles, two on each side, hanging in a large frame cemented into the ground. It allowed the four poles to move in concert, causing the plank to glide back and forth.

Like the bench ride at Willow Park, this ride could be quite relaxing when ridden at a slow to moderate speed; however, also like the bench ride, in the hands of one of Ashland's numerous teenage psychopaths, this ride was transformed into Satan's own death machine. Imagine a young boy about eight or nine enjoying a nice casual glide back and forth wearing shorts on a warm spring day. Suddenly, two feral, knuckle-dragging teenage boys jump on the ride, one on each end, with the young boy sitting and straddling the plank in the middle.

The two crazies are both standing at the ends of the plank with their hands gripping the poles, laughing and grinning like the lunatic hyenas they are. Rapidly, the plank moves faster and faster, then higher and higher. The poor boy in the middle is hanging onto the plank for dear life, trying desperately not to fall off. He is bent forward, gripping the plank tighter with his hands, and his legs are squeezing the thing as the wind whips at his hair and face. He can feel himself getting splinters in his hands and exposed legs, yet he hangs on desperately, knowing if he lets go, he'll likely fly off and die a horrible, disfiguring death. All the while, the maniacal demons at both ends of the board are roaring with pleasure.

The plank is traveling so high now the two juvenile delinquents are almost horizontal when the ride is at its apex. Just when the young boy is sure he can hold on no longer, he hears someone shouting, "Hey, you three. Knock it off before someone gets hurt."

Saved by an adult. Wait a minute. Did he say "three"? I'm the victim here. I'm not with these juvenile delinquents. You know what? I don't care. It doesn't matter to me if you lump me with those two psychopaths. All that matters to me is that I'm still alive and off that plank of death.

He can feel himself getting splinters in his hands and exposed legs, yet he hangs on desperately, knowing if he lets go, he'll likely fly off and die a horrible, disfiguring death.

There were a few other smaller parks in town as well, such as one on Stormy Hill and another down on Oakland Avenue, but I never frequented these or others. I can only assume they were perhaps even less maintained. In seeing pictures of the old parks where I used to play, my grandkids ask how we ever managed to survive. I reply with a line borrowed from comedian Brad Upton: "The dumb ones didn't make it."

Chapter 7

Many of the houses in Schuylkill County originated as what were called "company" houses. These were basic wood-framed row homes built by the coal companies originally to house mine workers and their families. The house where I grew up was part of a row of four small and narrow wood-framed houses. My house was about eleven or twelve feet wide and three similarly sized rectangular rooms deep. There were three rooms downstairs, three small bedrooms, and a bathroom upstairs.

The house was three stories tall in the front but only two in the back. To access the main floor from the front, you had to walk up steps to the raised front porch, which sat atop the coal bin. The coal bin had an outside access door, eventually leading to the cellar door and the cellar under the house. A small flip-open window about a foot square was located just under the porch at the highest point on the face of the coal bin. That window was used by the coal delivery trucks to place their coal shoots to fill the bin with coal.

As you entered that cellar door from the street, you would see to your right a series of ten-inch wide by one-inch-thick long boards stacked edge-to-edge and held in position by vertical wooden channels mounted on each side of the wall. These removable boards were meant to keep the coal in the bin while allowing access to the cellar. Over the winter, as the coal was consumed and the level dropped, boards could be removed one at a time to give easier access to the remaining supply.

By summertime, all the boards were removed, and all the coal was gone. This made for a cool place to hang out with other kids, tell scary stories, talk about movies, or just be a kid. Behind the coal bin was the main cellar that originally extended under only two rooms, but my dad, my brother, and I eventually dug out an additional space that ran under the kitchen in the back of the house. The area was the width and length of the kitchen above it and about eight feet deep. We hauled the dirt out in wheelbarrows, and I don't remember where or how we got rid of it. It was likely hauled up to the "strippins" and dumped there.

On the main floor of the house, the front room was what we called our parlor. It was about twelve feet square and could fit a chair, a sofa, an upright piano, and an end table or two. This parlor was located directly under my parents' bedroom. As a pre-teenager, I would watch TV in the parlor with my mom. My dad got up for work every morning at around 4:00, so he needed to get to sleep early. Often, we would have the TV playing louder than we should have.

This was back when we all had landline telephones, and you could call your own number. As a side note, my friend's dad was hard of hearing, and he lived about a block away. My dad had a great sense of humor, even when angry about something. So, when my dad wanted to tell us to turn down the TV, he would call our home phone. When my mom answered, my dad would say, "Hey! This is your neighbor from up on the hill; turn your damn TV down!" The irony of a half-deaf man who lived a block away calling to complain about noise was not lost on us. And to think people wonder where I get my sarcastic wit.

We always seemed to have an old, used piano in our parlor. I never knew where my dad got them, but they were all usually a bit out of tune. But we were grateful for them, and they met our needs. During the summer, I took free piano lessons with the high school music teacher at the high school behind our house.

I never advanced very far for two reasons. First, I never practiced my lessons, and second, I just wanted to bang on the keys, figuring out my own tunes by ear. So, I started over with the same introductory book every year and usually quit after a few weeks. Although I became quite good at playing the simple, three-note tune "Oscar the Octopus" with my right hand only, that, unfortunately, was the extent of my piano skills; however, I continued to pound the keys for a few years until I discovered I liked playing guitar much better.

The middle room was what we called our living room. It had a table, a sofa and a chair. It might have been twelve feet by thirteen feet, by my recollection. My dad had built a small closet off of this room, which held all of our coats, boots, toys, and pretty much everything else. This was quite an accomplishment, considering that the lone closet had to accommodate all six family members. The cellar access door was in the short hallway between the parlor and the living room, under the stairs leading to the upper level.

The next room was the kitchen, about the same size as the living room. When I was small, all of our cabinets were white-painted metal. Eventually, my dad built new wooden cabinets to replace these metal antiquities. There was originally a coal stove in the kitchen, but that was ultimately replaced with a gas stove fed by an external propane tank until the gas company eventually ran a line to our house.

Our kitchen table, located next to the back door, was a typical metal and Formica top table like you see in pictures from that era. Our eating area was small, but somehow, we all managed to fit in at the table for every meal. I was and still am a picky eater; however, this was a time of parents chanting, "Children are starving in China, so you can't leave the table until you eat everything on your plate." I spent far too many nights with tears streaming down my young cheeks, forcing food I hated that had unfortunately cooled into my unwilling mouth and reluctantly swallowing it.

I eventually developed what I thought to be an ingenious technique to deceive my parents into thinking I had cleaned my plate. When I only had a little bit left, I would hide things I didn't like, such as bread crusts, onions, and other vegetables, under the rim of my plate. When you looked at my plate, it appeared to be scraped clean. I would get up and run from the table. Little did I realize that when my mom picked up my plate from the table, she would find my remnants in a perfectly circular pattern under the plate. I actually thought I was getting away with something when all the while, my mom was probably busy laughing at my creative but stupid solution.

Dinner was also a time when I got to crack a lot of goofy jokes, again in an attempt to deflect everyone from the fact that I was only eating what I liked and hiding the rest. Dad was always yelling at me and my antics, fearing that I might someday grow up to be, as he called it, "the class clown." Looking back, I have no idea what would have been wrong with that label. It's good to make people laugh, right? My sister Jeanie loved my goofy antics and spent most nights laughing at my performances. Mom would tell Jeanie to "stop encouraging him," yet she was smiling and trying to control her own laughter.

I had a lot of memories of that small kitchen and that crowded table. Somewhere along the line, it was replaced with a wooden set. Then, when I was in my early teens, my dad remodeled our kitchen with cabinets he built, and we got an L-shaped kitchen nook from Sears to replace the wooden table and chair set. It was not as much fun as the old table, probably because my two older sisters had married and moved out by then. It's hard to be funny when your number one fan has left the building.

That kitchen always seemed very narrow, which it was and might not be desirable by today's standards. As things turned out, having a long, thin kitchen probably saved my younger brother George's life.

One day, when George was maybe five or six years old, he must have wanted something on the top shelf or perhaps in the freezer section of our refrigerator. He couldn't reach it, but he could climb. So, he opened the door and, using the shelves, he began to climb. In doing so, he accidentally pulled the refrigerator over on himself. He dropped to the floor directly in the path of the falling refrigerator. If we had a wider kitchen, he would have been crushed. But the fridge fell against the opposite counter and cabinets, and George was bombarded with milk, eggs, and other products from the open door.

As I mentioned earlier, our kitchen originally sat on top of a bed of dirt at the back of the cellar. There was a small crawlspace that allowed minimal access to plumbing. Unfortunately, it also permitted insects and rats to have access to our kitchen. One of the more prevalent species of crawling menaces were the aforementioned critters — those disgusting water bugs/cockroaches of the large, black, and shiny variety.

These creatures and the occasional rat entering our kitchen base cabinets were why we eventually dug out the back cellar and built concrete foundation walls, giving our cellar an additional room and eliminating the pest problem.

Off of the living room, there was a set of stairs leading to the upstairs. At the top to the right was my parents' bedroom, which was the same size as the parlor. To the left was a long hallway which passed by a central bedroom and a bathroom and eventually led to a third bedroom.

Originally, there was no hallway, and you had to walk through the open center bedroom to get to the back room. This made for little privacy for whoever occupied the middle space. So, once again, my dad was put to work, and he built a wall with a door, forming both a hallway and a private bedroom shared by my two older sisters, Louiseann and Georgine.

George and I shared the back bedroom, which only had room for a single bed and a small dresser. Eventually, as my brother and I grew, my parents got us bunk beds. The girls had twin beds in their room. When I was about nine or ten, my Italian grandfather, Pietro

Malafarina, came to live with us for a while. That was before my dad built the wall for the center bedroom.

If I remember correctly, Pap slept in the back room during his stay, which meant all four of us kids had to be crammed into the middle bedroom for a while. George's and my beds were capable of bunking, which might help explain how we all fit into that space. Again, my memory of that time is fuzzy. Then again, it was also possible this happened before we could afford the bunk beds, and there may have been two regular-sized beds in the room, one for the girls and one for the boys. I recall a small dresser was in the open center room against the neighboring wall. I remember my mom cautioning me to be sure to close the drawers because Grandpap couldn't see well and might trip over an open drawer.

I also recall Grandpap playing checkers with my brother, who might have been four or five at the time. He tricked George by putting the red checkers on the red spaces and the black ones on the black squares. This made for strange results. They would play for hours, and no one ever lost a piece.

What I recall best is Grandpap teaching me swear words in Italian. I've forgotten most of them but still recall "chooch bruto," which I was told meant "dumb jackass." I also remember "cacca pantaloni" which meant someone who crapped in his own pants.

But I digress. The bathroom in our house was quite small, with room for a cast iron claw-foot tub, a sink, and a toilet. It was located between the middle bedroom and the back bedroom. The hall leading from the stairs to my bedroom at the back of the house was always a scary place at night for a young kid like me with an overactive imagination and a love of all things horror-related. One of my short stories, *The Lurkers*, uses that upstairs hallway as its focal point.

I should point out here that, although I had no idea as a young boy that I would grow up to eventually write horror stories, I should have seen it coming. I have always had a love/hate relationship with the genre. My bedroom was filled with horror memorabilia, much to the chagrin of my younger brother, who hated horror as a kid. I bought and assembled most of the Aurora Universal Monsters models, Frankenstein, Wolfman, Dracula, Phantom of the Opera, and others. I even had a customizing kit with rats, snakes, tombstones, and such that I could add to the standard models to make them unique.

For one of my birthdays, or perhaps Christmas, my parents bought me a model called Big Franky, which was a replica of Frankenstein's monster that stood about two feet tall and had movable arms. It was my prized possession and was quite scary on a dark night. It was the inspiration for yet another of my short stories, aptly named *Big Frankie*. Back then, there was one thing you could count on — if it was scary, you would probably find it in my bedroom.

Regarding the love/hate thing I had for the horror genre, I loved collecting horror memorabilia and going to the Roxy Theater to watch old horror movies. I loved horror magazines whenever I could afford to buy one. However, in the dark of night, I slept with the covers pulled over my head, somehow living under the delusion that the thin fabric would protect me from the evil monsters as I slumbered. I suppose you could call that behavior the ostrich syndrome. That was the hate part of the equation. Eventually, that childhood terror and my imagination combined to create an adult who would lose the fear but continue to love the imaginative part of that relationship with horror his entire life.

However, in the dark of night, I slept with the covers pulled over my head, somehow living under the delusion that the thin fabric would protect me from the evil monsters as I slumbered.

Back to the house. Earlier, I mentioned the coal-fired Heatrola that forced heat from the cellar up to the first floor through metal grates and, if luck was with us, through upstairs registers to the bedrooms.

56

You may wonder how well this system worked. The short answer would be it was neither effective nor efficient. In the winter, we all slept with flannel pajamas and lots of covers. In the morning, we kids took turns standing on the downstairs register to stay warm as we dressed for school. Eventually, my parents could afford to disconnect the coal furnace and replace it with baseboard electric heat. I can't recall if the monstrosity was ever removed, but knowing my dad, he probably kept it around as a backup heat source "just in case." He was never one to go through life without a backup plan. I have followed in his footsteps and always have a backup plan for almost every situation. When plan "A" fails, go on to plan "B."

Having been in many coal region row homes in my life, I can safely say that although some were larger and some smaller, they all were very similar to mine. Another interesting thing was that, unlike modern homes, the plumbing in many of these older homes ran outside the walls, exposed to the living space, not inside the walls. This was probably because when the homes were originally built as company houses, they had no indoor plumbing, and many had outhouses for bathrooms. So, when plumbing was added, the pipes were usually placed in the corners of the rooms, running upward from floor to floor.

In the early days, seeing these pipes inside your house was likely a positive thing as it showed the early 20th-century homeowner was affluent enough to have indoor plumbing. Seeing these pipes in a home might have been a status symbol; however, later generations began to view them as eyesores. Eventually, people managed to find creative ways to deal with these exposed pipes. If people chose to wallpaper their rooms, a common practice was to wrap the exposed pipes in the same wallpaper. The idea was to camouflage the pipes to have them blend in with the walls and become almost invisible. Other people would build boxes around the pipes and either paper or panel the walls and the new boxed-in areas.

Many Skook homes were small, and many Skook families had four or more kids. Although money was tight, material items were never affordable, and privacy was as rare as a good-paying job, Schuylkill County families always found ways to create bonds of love and respect that lasted a lifetime.

Chapter 8

The neighborhood was the center of every kid's universe in small Schuylkill County towns. It was where we lived and played during the summer, from early morning until the street lights came on at night. When we were younger, we never left the neighborhood and were always within the sound of our mothers' voices. Then again, there was no need to leave the neighborhood as it had everything we needed and plenty of other kids to share our time with.

Our summer routine was always the same. We woke up, ate breakfast, and then went outside. We knew it was lunchtime when we heard someone's mother calling his name. The same was true for supper, although a working father might have arrived home and sometimes called. After dinner, we were back outside until the street lights came on. As we got older, we could stay out after dark and play in the dark until bedtime.

There were dozens of neighborhoods in most towns, and because we all went to school together, we knew who lived in what part of town and in what neighborhood. As we grew and expanded our world, we often invited kids from other areas to play on our street. Likewise, we would go to different neighborhoods on occasion. But for the most part, we stayed where we were most comfortable and spent time with the neighborhood kids we knew best.

Whenever I take what my wife calls my "pilgrimage to Mecca," my trip back to the old neighborhood, and I see how small the area was, I marvel at how it seemed like so much more to me during those early years. As kids, we never seemed to run out of fun things to do in that amazing little world.

The portion of Arch Street where I grew up only spanned the distance of one block between 8th and 9th Street. The next parallel street in the southerly direction was Market Street. The backyards of the houses on Market Street butted against Arch Street. Since Market Street was wider and had more traffic than little Arch Street, most kids from both streets usually met on Arch. Here is our section of Arch Street as it appears today.

We usually used North Ninth Street for our whiffle ball or touch football games despite its traffic because it was relatively flat.

Whenever someone yelled "car," our game would be temporarily interrupted until the car passed, and then it was back to action. Ninth Street was usually quite busy, and "car" was shouted more times than we preferred.

Here is a shot of North Ninth Street today.

Our neighborhood was located at the northern end of town, with the Ashland High School building behind us and nothing beyond that but a vast wasteland of abandoned strip mines and, eventually, the town of Centralia. At one time, you could drive up Catawissa Road and get to Centralia, but for as long as I can remember, the road dead-ended at the strip mine pits. If you wanted to get to Centralia by car, you had to do so by State Route 61. You could walk there if you felt like taking the scenic route through the strippins by adventuring through "brache holes," which is what we called the enormous pits left by strip mining.

Another ecological nightmare left by the days of mining was the "sulfur cricks" which were creeks and streams that had turned bright orange from sulfuric mine waste. When I was little, I had no idea that all creeks weren't orange and didn't smell like farts. We were, however, smart enough to never try to drink from any of them. There's something about bright orange scum on top of the water that tells even the dumbest of the dumb kids that drinking the stuff probably wasn't the best idea. Then again, that was a time when people knew, even without warning labels, that coffee was hot and shouldn't be spilled on your lap.

When we were still small, like five or six years old, one of the neighborhood kids, I believe it was Eric, got an idea that we should do a sort of Halloween trick-or-treat thing over the summer. We decided to call it a raid. So, one hot July day, several of us dug out our Halloween costumes and went around knocking on neighbors' doors. When they opened their doors, we said, "This is a raid!" Some folks laughed, some shut their doors on us, but a few gave us treats. The idea was a flop as we didn't get many treats, and we sweated profusely in those costumes in July. But we had fun, so I suppose that was something.

We spent a lot of time during the summer discussing TV shows and horror movies that we saw. Sometimes, we would share jokes or scary stories. Most of the time, we hung out, made up games, rode our bikes, and we built tree shacks with nails and tools confiscated from our dads and scrap lumber scavenged from wherever we could find it. We seemed to build new tree shacks in different trees at different locations throughout the woods every year.

We experimented with building "jitneys" as we got older, around ten or twelve. We usually had to enlist our fathers' help for these endeavors for several reasons. The most obvious reason was that we had few of the skills required, no technical knowledge, and no way to acquire the materials we needed.

These were about as primitive as you might imagine; at least, they started out that way. Our dads would get us a two-inch by ten-inch piece of scrap planking about four or five feet long. I have no idea why, but it seemed most dads had planks lying around. It was just a fact of life in the Skook. There were no home centers like Lowe's or Home Depot, and even if there were, we couldn't afford to buy what we needed.

Next, we had to find wheels and axles. Each jitney would require a minimum of four wheels and two axles. This usually meant a trip to the local dump or, more likely, a walk up to the strippins, where we could often find abandoned baby carriages. These were usually dumped because the upholstery was ripped or the insides worn out. Most of the time, the undercarriage and wheels were fine. Once we had the baby buggy, it was simply a matter of removing the wheels and axles, sanding off any rust, and giving them some oil to bring them back to life.

The back axle was mounted to a short piece of two-by-four by feeding the axle through a couple of bent-over nails. That assembly was then nailed to the bottom of the plank. The same axle process was repeated for the front, but that two-by-four wasn't fixed to the front of the plank. A hole was drilled through the center of the wood with a mating hole drilled in the plank. This was accomplished manually using a brace and bit hand drill. Then, a bolt with washers strategically positioned was fed through the holes, allowing the bottom front piece to pivot. By nailing a rope to both sides of the lower front two-by-four, extending out beyond the plank, we had the ability to steer.

This is usually as far as we went with these early prototypes. Breaking was typically accomplished by dragging one's feet, Fred Flintstone style. As our skills increased, sometimes a piece of wood bolted to the side of the plank could be pushed, pivoting its lower end against one of the back tires to help slow the jitney down and simultaneously increase sneaker life. Eventually, some of the more sophisticated jitneys had steering wheel capabilities using a crate, broomstick handles, or metal rods along with wire and pulleys. Everybody seemed to have old steering wheels lying around, too. Again, I have no idea why this was the case either.

My dad owned a Ford van, which he used to transport several factory coworkers fifty miles to Reading and back daily. The van had a steering wheel positioned almost horizontally rather than the traditional angled orientation. This was one of those vans with the engine between the two front seats. It looked like pictures of city buses or the school buses we had ridden in. This inspired my dad to rig my jitney with a complex series of wires, small pulleys, and a steering wheel positioned like his van. It worked, but what had been my super cool, although primitive, racing jitney now looked like public transportation. I never let my dad know I wasn't a fan of his creation. Criticizing his work was something I never would have considered doing. He was so proud of what he had accomplished.

Another thing all of us neighborhood kids loved was fire. It seemed we always had easy access to open flames. I know that sounds ludicrous in today's world of coddling our kids, but that's how it was. And we took every opportunity to turn any open flame into a good time. One of our most easily accessible sources of fire were things known as smudge pots.

Whenever any roadwork or utility work causing a potentially unsafe driving or walking hazard existed, those responsible took precautions to protect people from tripping, falling, or damaging their cars. This was accomplished by placing a black and white striped wooden sawhorse over the offensive hole. But here's where the fun begins. Although people could easily see the sawhorse in the daylight, what about at night? Enter every kid's dream come true — the smudge pot.

A smudge pot was a ball-shaped metal canister filled with oil or kerosene, hung with wires from the cross member of the sawhorse, and ignited at night so people could see the potential hazard. However, at the time, we had no idea what it was called, so we either referred to it in Skook Speak as "onea dem der round hangin' tings" or sometimes used the more accurately descriptive name, "cannonball." This later name was spot on because the thing looked like every cannonball ever seen on Saturday morning cartoons, from Bugs Bunny to the Roadrunner. For a neighborhood full of junior pyromaniacs, the smudge pot was an irresistible attraction. Like cavemen, we were drawn to the open flame at the top of the smudge pot. It was like a gift from the gods. Fire was at our eager fingertips any night we wanted it. No, sir, we didn't have to steal our dad's matches or lighters. If someone had a punk stick to light, cannonball to the rescue. Firecrackers or bottle rockets? No problem. Light it up on "onea dem der round hangin' tings."

For a neighborhood full of junior pyromaniacs, smudge pots were an irresistible attraction.

One of my older friends had put together a model car with wheels that rotated; I think it was Eddie. It was probably a '56 Chevy model. It seemed every kid at some point in time back then built a '56 or '57 Chevy model. As it worked out, there was a sawhorse with a smudge pot a good distance up the Catawissa Road hill. He got the awesome idea to take his model up, set it on fire, and roll it all the way down the hill in the dark. This idea was fraught with potential disaster, but somehow, he pulled it off without starting a brush fire, burning down any houses, or exploding anyone's car. Watching that flaming model fly down the hill, dripping melted plastic in its wake, was truly a most incredible sight for young eyes.

But smudge pots were only one source of flaming fun in our neighborhood. Next to the high school behind our house, the school had built an incinerator for burning paper waste. It was only a five-by-seven cement block rectangle. It had an opening in the front and was open on top. The cool thing about it was that the path leading to the high school baseball field not only went right past the incinerator but also allowed the pedestrian to be above the burning debris.

Today, it would have been considered a safety hazard as anyone walking by could easily have slipped and fallen into the fire pit. The school would probably be required to have a fence around it and a screen on top. But in a neighborhood abundant with young, fledgling firebugs, this thing was a source of wonder. It was common for us to gather there and not only stare longingly into the dancing flames and sniff the smoldering reams of old classroom papers but also to toss in our own wood and paper sacrifices to the gods of the fiery pit.

Amazingly, none of us were ever hurt. As hypnotic as the burning paper was, we also kept a close eye on the incinerator for the time before the janitor started the fire. That was when he filled it up. That was when there was a potential treasure trove waiting to be scavenged.

This was a senior high school where teachers confiscated all sorts of things from their students during the school year. What they took eventually ended up in the burn pile. The key was to get into the incinerator through the front entrance, sift through the debris, and try to find something valuable. For example, sometimes we scored *Mad* magazines or even *Hot Rod* magazines. On rare occasions, we might discover the greatest of all great finds, a *Playboy* magazine. Considering all we could traditionally hope for was a *National Geographic* with some topless natives, snagging a *Playboy* was like finding the Un-Holy Grail.

One day, we climbed into the incinerator and found a shoebox. We lifted the lid and were so overcome with elation we could scarcely control our emotions. This was the big strike, the type of score we could only fantasize about. It was the mother load. No, it wasn't a dirty magazine or playing cards with naked women on them. Inside the shoebox were more than a dozen beautiful, plastic, translucent water pistols in all the favorite colors: orange, yellow, and green. One or more of the teachers must have confiscated these and saved them throughout the school year. Now, they were waiting either for a fiery end or to be rescued by a bunch of boys who knew exactly what to do with them.

Our neighborhood was an amazing place for a kid to be a kid and have more fun than most people could imagine. Later, I'll tell you about the strange games we invented to entertain ourselves. But first, I'd like to discuss Skook wildlife.

Chapter 9

Something my neighborhood seemed to have an abundance of were rats and feral cats. Our neighborhood backed up against wild, wooded areas, which led to abandoned strip mines that were illegal dumping sites where rats flourished. Things would have been fine had the rats stayed up in the strippins, but they weren't content to stay there. They preferred to live in and under garages and coal sheds. When they were not going from one open sewer grate to another, they could often be found scavenging in neighborhood trash.

This was a time before plastic trash cans when many cans were made of heavy-gauge galvanized steel. As long as the lid was tightly fitting, the rats couldn't get to your garbage. But if the top was loose or missing, the trash inside became a buffet for these monsters, and monsters they were. They were often two or three times the size of a typical rat and five times as nasty, and they reproduced like...well, like rats.

Our backyard was not very big. It might have been twelve feet wide and maybe double that in length. At the rear of our yard was a former coal shanty that we used to store things we couldn't fit in the house or cellar. Items like shovels, rakes, pitchforks, and the like. Occasionally, I would move some of the stuff around, clear a path inside, and pretend it was my clubhouse.

Our neighbor's rickety old garage was between our house and the shed on the left side of the yard. It probably should have been torn down, and honestly, I doubt our neighbors were using it for anything. That is to say, our human neighbors. However, we had a whole bunch of neighbors living in that garage that didn't come close to qualifying as human. These were rats, and there were a lot of them.

Being the resourceful type and owning a .22-caliber rifle, my dad decided it was time he dealt with this rat problem personally. My dad had been teaching me to shoot for several years, probably since I was six or seven. I'm sure this was comical to watch since the rifle was longer than I was tall. Dad wanted me to understand gun safety and have both a respect for firearms and a knowledge of just how dangerous they could be if mishandled.

Now, before we get into a pro-gun/anti-gun debate, I should point out that my dad instilled in me such an understanding of what guns can do that, as an adult, I want nothing to do with them. I have no desire to take away anyone else's right to own a gun. But for me, it's probably best if I avoid them. You see, I'm kind of a klutz, and I know it. Okay, saying I'm "kind of" a klutz is like someone saying they're "kind of pregnant." I'm careless and easily distracted. If I was a superhero, I'd have to call myself, The Spastic Warrior. I'm the last person you want anywhere near a firearm. I would likely be voted "most likely to shoot himself in the foot."

The awkwardness started when I was a pre-teen and has stayed with me since then. In seventh grade, we were given eye-hand coordination tests, which I believe were sponsored by the government. I failed every test miserably.

Regarding target shooting, things were different when I was a little kid, and my dad watched my every move and guided me when shooting. Back then, I actually became a pretty good shot for a while. Dad would take me target shooting up in the strippins behind our house. We would pick up bottles, plates, glassware, and anything we thought would make a good target and stand them up in a line. Then we'd shoot them.

Dad was friends with the chief of police in town then, and he told him about the rat problem. He asked the chief if shooting the rats that came into our yard would be okay. After some discussion, it was "unofficially" determined that since we lived at the edge of town with no houses behind us, it would be ok if no one was nearby. Even though the high school was behind our house, the building was off to the left of our property; also, school was out for summer vacation, so no students were around, especially on Saturdays or Sundays.

As far as that "okay" went, it was so unofficial that we were lucky no one ever complained or put the "permission" to the test. I suspect if someone had complained, that "permission" would have vanished into thin air. So, for several Sunday afternoons in the summer, Dad sat at my bedroom window, which was open a few inches, waiting for the rats to show themselves. He managed to shoot quite a few of them. Then he gave me a turn, reminding me of everything he had taught me. Then he told me when a rat finally came out into our yard, I should aim my shot directly in front of the rat's nose.

He said rats were extremely fast and sprang forward when they heard the shot. He said he used this technique with his shots, which was why he got several of them. Who was I to argue? So, there I was, waiting at the window with my dad watching me, hoping for a rat to show his ugly face. Now, if this were a movie, here would be where the rat came out, but being too kindhearted, I'd refused to shoot the poor, innocent creature. (Cue heartwarming music score.) But this was reality, and although I never hunted and have no interest in doing so now, back then, I wanted nothing more than to blow that vile critter's head off.

To answer the question I'm sure you're asking, did I shoot one? The truth is, I can't remember. I want to say I was such an amazing marksman that I put one right through his rodent brain. However, it was more likely that I missed it, and the rat scurried back to his home under the old garage. I suppose the point is that I tried, and that was something.

As I recall, we did this for a few Sundays until the rats got wise to us, and we assumed they left the garage, although that was not what happened. I suspect they were being hunted by the mountain cats, which we'll discuss shortly.

Before that, there was a funny story about my dad and our Sunday afternoon rat safaris. One Sunday, when we were ready to call it quits for the day, my mom came up to my bedroom and asked if it was a good idea for me to participate in this activity. Dad told her it was perfectly safe, and his gun wasn't loaded. Thankfully, the barrel was pointed upwards because when he pulled the trigger, the gun went off, and a .22-caliber bullet put a small hole in my bedroom ceiling. So, yeah, the only reason this story is funny is because no one was hurt. That hole remained in my ceiling for years to come. I think Mom wouldn't let Dad fix it just so she could remind him of what he had done and what could have happened. But now let's discuss those mountain cats.

The mountain cats that stalked our neighborhood were most definitely feral; however, they were so much more than wild and worse than savage. That's why we called them mountain cats. They lived and flourished in the mountains and garbage-filled strip mines outside town, behind our house. What was worse was they were huge, strong, and wild, and they would attack if they felt threatened.

When they decided to come down from the hills in search of food, they came in packs, like wild dogs. They were two or three times the size of a typical house cat and rippled with feline muscles from generations of Darwinian survival in the wilderness. On more than one occasion, they stalked me as I walked home from the Roxy Theater at night. I threw rocks at them to scare them away, but they never flinched. I could only scare them away if I got lucky and hit the biggest. Then they would slink off into the darkness, and I'd run my sorry butt home.

Often, groups of three or more neighborhood kids would get together, look for a cluster of these cats, and bombard them with rocks until they ran back into the hills. But they would always eventually return.

My dad decided that the "permission" he had been informally given to shoot rats also extended to mountain cats. When I say these cats were big and strong, here is an example of what they could do. One day, we heard a deep growling coming from our backyard. One of the mountain cats was perched on top of our fence post, howling. Our neighbor had a female cat, and I suspect the beast was looking to romance her with his machismo. He had the look of a savage predator in his eyes. The fence post was about six inches square and four feet high. The monster barely fit on the flat top of it and rose above it for another two to three feet.

This was all the motivation my dad needed. He went upstairs, grabbed his rifle, and opened my bedroom window. The cat looked defiantly up at him without an ounce of fear as the window slid open. It was like the beast was daring my dad to try and stop him. Dad took him up on the challenge and shot the thing right between the eyes. I wouldn't have believed what happened next had I not seen it myself.

Instead of falling dead, the cat flipped backward through the air in an impact-induced somersault and landed on the ground on all fours. Then, with a .22-shell bouncing around inside the cat's massive skull, the beast took off, leaving a trail of blood behind him. Dad put his rifle away and then tried to track down the mountain cat. He followed the blood trail and eventually found the thing dead more than two blocks away. It was a massive beast with a head twice the size of any house cat I had ever seen.

I don't recall how many more of these creatures my dad shot, but I'm sure there were more. Eventually, the cats left the neighborhood and went back to the mountains. Shortly after, we got a dog who loved catching rats in our backyard. We called him Spot, and he was a mix of beagle and who-done-it. He was a regular Heinz 57 variety sort of breed, as people called mutts back then. We built him a doghouse where he often would lie in wait for the opportunity to ring one of the rodents' necks. Maybe he helped to chase the cats away as well.

Many years later, when Spot moved on to the great water dish in the sky, Dad asked me to help him flip over the doghouse so we could break it up and get rid of it. When we pushed the thing over, we saw the back end of a rat with its whipping tail diving into a hole in the ground that had been dug directly under our doghouse.

"Where there's one, there's more," Dad said as he handed me a shovel. "Stay here. I'll be right back. If a rat pokes his head out, whack him with that shovel."

I assumed Dad was going in to get his rifle, but to my surprise, he came out carrying a large double-handled soup pot. I could see the steam rising up from its contents. Dad said, "Be ready with the shovel."

I was thinking, "Ready for what?" I had no idea what he was about to do.

Remember, I was a young teenager then, and looking back, I wasn't very good at recognizing the obvious. I've always lived in my own world, and sometimes I have a tendency to miss what is right in front of my face. This was one of those times. I remember Dad walking over to the hole in the dirt, and before my brain could comprehend what he would do, Dad poured the pot full of boiling water down into the hole. Then he grabbed a pitchfork.

Nothing happened for a few seconds, and then we heard high-pitched squealing as rat after rat came up from the hole. "Now get' 'em!" Dad shouted.

Not thinking, just reacting, I started smashing the creatures with my shovel. At first, two adult-sized rats came out, and then about ten smaller ones. It was a slaughter. I beat rat after rat, and Dad used the pitchfork to make rodent shish kabobs. At one point in the chaos, a rat ran up the handle of Dad's pitchfork, and he flicked it off. It flew through the air, right past my face, nearly hitting me, but landed in our neighbor's Dalmatian's fenced-in pen. The dog, whose name I believe was Prince, made short work of the rat as we finished with the others.

When it was said and done, about eleven rats of various sizes either lay dead on the ground or their carcasses dangled from the tines of Dad's pitchfork. I suppose I should have been sick or upset by what happened, but I took it all in stride, as I recall. After all, it was just another day of growin' up Skook.

After the incident with the mountain cat, word got around the neighborhood that Dad had a gun and shot pests. That was when my dad was approached by one of our neighbors, who I'll call Bill. Bill told my dad he had a sick dog that needed to be put down, and he asked if Dad would be willing to do the deed. Here's the account, as Dad told it to me.

Dad refused to shoot Bill's dog at first and even offered to lend Bill his gun, but Bill said he didn't have the stomach for something like that. Still, my dad refused. Then Bill pleaded, saying the dog was suffering and this was the right thing to do; he just couldn't do it himself.

Something you should know about my dad. He may have had his gruff side and cursed like the factory worker he was, but he was also a kind and caring man who would give the proverbial shirt off his back to a friend in need. He did, however, suffer from what I call Malafarina men's disease. In my life-long observations of my male Malafarina uncles, my cousins, myself, and my brother, if you employ us, pay us well, treat us with respect, and ask for our help, you will get more than your money's worth.

On the other hand, if you demand, threaten, cajole, or try to con us in a feeble attempt to force us to do something we don't feel comfortable doing or simply don't want to do, you will see a completely different and unpleasant side of us appear. We don't always get visibly angry, but we always get even, often in passive-aggressive ways you never will see coming. Bill put my dad in such a situation by trying to guilt him into the unpleasant task.

Finally, Dad reluctantly relented, but only if Bill agreed to come along to help with the animal. Dad explained that he didn't know the dog and didn't want to risk getting bitten or having the dog get away. Plus, Dad didn't want to deal with getting rid of a dead dog carcass. So, Bill and my dad eventually took the animal up into the hills behind our house near the abandoned strip mines and found a place to do the deed.

Dad said he had Bill tie the dog to a tree so he couldn't move around much. He wanted this unpleasant business to be over quickly, preferably with one shot. When the dog was secure, Dad took aim, and Bill looked away, not wanting to see what was coming.

Just before Dad pulled the trigger, he shouted, "Bill, he's getting away!"

Bill turned to look, and my dad pulled the trigger and shot the dog. Bill stopped in his tracks, then turned and vomited in the dirt. I don't know if there's any moral to this story, but if there is, it might be don't make a Malafarina man feel cornered. If you do, then sooner or later, when you least expect it...expect it.

Chapter 10

In the area behind our house, across from the side entrance to the high school, was a place we affectionately called "The Pines." It was a long, steep forest hillside that connected the lower road next to the high school with Catawissa Road. For many of us neighborhood kids, it was a place of awe and mystery, an almost enchanted fantasy forest, a world in which we could disappear.

The Pines were populated with dozens of decades-old pine trees that reached far into the sky, farther than most of us could climb. The lower branches were trimmed, but higher up, they grew thick, connected with other trees, and formed a darkening and cooling canopy. It was one of our go-to places to beat the summer heat. The steeply sloped floor of the pines was blanketed with several inches of fallen pine needles, making for a soft place to sit.

But much better than just a soft and comfortable place to relax, these needles, combined with the steep grade of The Pines, provided an incredible thirty or more foot-long slide. All it took was a cardboard box broken down flat, and you were good to go.

We would stop by the state-run liquor store on the north side of Centre Street just down from the Marko Town House and ask the man behind the counter for some empty boxes. We never wondered if it was okay for little kids to go into the liquor store; it was just something we always did. If our moms needed boxes for packing stuff, they'd send us to the state store. The guy would go into the back and come out with a box for each of us. They were good, heavy things made of multiple layers of cardboard, strong enough to carry full liquor bottles.

Once, when my mom needed some boxes, I got the bright idea to ride my bike to the liquor store. The store was only a few short blocks away, but it might as well have been miles away in my young, lazy mind. Since I did use my bike, I could only bring home two boxes. I gripped each one by a flap hanging from my handlebars.

About a block from my house on North Ninth Street, one of the boxes got entangled in my front wheel spokes, jamming it in place and sending me flying over the handlebars. My head hit the center nut, holding the handlebars as I passed through, tearing a flap of skin at the top of my forehead. Although it was just a superficial scalp wound, I bled like crazy, and I eventually needed a trip to the hospital and four stitches. I suspect, by the looks on the faces of the neighborhood kids who saw me doing my handlebar acrobatics, that I must have looked like something out of one of our horror movies.

I remember getting up and walking home a bit dazed. Some of the kids grabbed the bike and boxes and brought them home for me. I recall my mom calmly leading me to the kitchen, sitting me on a chair, and washing my face to determine where I was cut. Most of that is a blur for me, except when my sister, Jeanie, came into the kitchen, seeing me in all my crimson-dripping glory.

Jeanie always had a tendency to exaggerate and overdramatize reality. Remember I said I only had a scalp wound, not a skull fracture? When Jeanie came running into the kitchen, seeing the flap of skin and all the blood, she immediately and quite hysterically began shouting, "I can see his brains! His brains are spilling out his head!"

Luckily, I have never been the type to get too excited about things. Between that and seeing my mom roll her eyes in a dismissive, "You know you sister" expression, I remained calm. I was patched up at the hospital as good as new. Apparently, sometimes, the dumb ones do make it. That being the case, I learned my lesson the hard way and never took my bike to the liquor store again.

But I eventually returned for more boxes because they worked great for sliding down The Pines. We would struggle to climb up the slippery slope by holding our cardboard box in one hand while using the other to grab roots and younger trees, pulling ourselves to the top. It would have been much safer had we chosen to walk along the connecting streets and then up Catawissa Road to get to the top of The Pines, but where was the fun in that? Maybe I should have hit my head harder on that bike flip and knocked more sense into it. Instead of the

76

path of least resistance, my friends and I always chose the course of more adventure and struggled up the slick bed of pine needles. Our reward was a lightning-fast, spinal column-abusing ride that lasted less than seven seconds but was well worth it.

Once we got to The Pines, we'd remove the inside grid of cardboard from our boxes; this was the stuff that kept the bottles from smashing together. Then we'd throw that into the high school incinerator. Next, we'd break down the back side of the box, giving us another twelve inches of sitting space. Imagine a box with three sides intact with a kid sitting inside, his feet facing the vertical front side and his backside resting on the broken-down rear flap of the box. This method all but guaranteed no pine needles would enter your box and inhibit your speed.

Eventually, after several trips, the front face of the box would crush and become less square and more rounded. This would make your sled more aerodynamic and improve your speed even more. Of course, the box would only survive so many trips down the hill until all the sides collapsed. When that happened, you had to fold over the two side panels onto the base, then pull up and hold onto the front panel, resembling a bobsled. You could continue to use the box for several more trips until it eventually fell apart and joined its other components in the incinerator.

The Pines is also where we learned to climb trees. Even though the first five feet or so were trimmed, these amazing trees had branch stubs about six inches to a foot long, poking out in various directions making a great starting point to get us to the upper fuller branches. Back then, I was a good climber, spending lots of time getting sap on my hands and clothes climbing those trees. I didn't realize my eyesight was bad, so when I climbed, I never realized how high up I was. When I turned sixteen and applied for my driving permit, I failed the eye test and had to get glasses. Suddenly, I could see things more clearly than I had ever imagined possible. It was a great gift that I hadn't even known I needed. But as they say, the Lord giveth and the Lord taketh away. Or, as my economics teacher once said, "You can't have everything. For everything you get, there is something you have to do without." The gift of clear eyesight was no exception. From that day on, I have had a paralyzing fear of heights since I could see the danger I was missing before.

The Pines was also a great place to hang out with friends. In the permanent shade of these majestic pine trees, you were guaranteed at least a ten-degree cooler temperature, perhaps more if there was a breeze.

Since the Catawissa Road hill was at the top edge of The Pines, the combination formed a great shortcut to quickly get off the mountain and put me right in the back of my house. This was important at lunchtime. When you happened to be up to no good at the top of the hill and heard your mom call you for lunch, you knew you had to get home quickly. A running slide down through The Pines was an awesome shortcut.

On occasion, I would go into The Pines alone to simply sit and think. This always ended badly for me. It should have been a calming and peaceful exercise, a type of meditation. However, with my active imagination combined with my love/hate relationship with horror, more often than not I would imagine some terrible creatures manifesting themselves from the dirt, needles, and sap and rising up to come for me.

When that happened, I had to slide down the pine needles on my backside and then run home, acting like all was right with the world, while being terrified to turn around and look back at The Pines, out of the fear I might see that golem looking at me and perhaps pointing his long finger at me, marking me for a painful and horrible death. It wasn't easy being me while Growin' up Skook.

I would imagine some terrible creatures manifesting themselves from the dirt, needles, and sap and rising up to come for me.

Chapter 11

Games were a big part of our lives when we were looking for ways to entertain ourselves over the long summer months. It was funny how, in the last few weeks of school, we planned all the things we couldn't wait to do when school was over; however, after the first few weeks, we usually struggled to find fun things to do that wouldn't get us into too much trouble.

We had all heard urban legends of kids who got in trouble and were sent off to "reform school." We had no idea if places like this really existed or if they were just stories adults made sure we heard about. Or maybe it was something we learned from watching reruns of the "Little Rascals." As kids, we imagined being sent off to a concentration-style camp where we would wear black and white striped uniforms with flat-topped billed caps and have a ball and chain attached to our ankles. We would be forced to work on the chain gang driving railroad spikes into ties next to Chinese coolie immigrants like on Bonanza, or else shoveling coal all day long as punishment for whatever our offenses might be. Looking back, I suspect reform school was no more a thing than "the poor house" was. It might have existed decades earlier, but it had been replaced by juvenile detention. Whatever the name, although we might have come dangerously close a time or two, none of us was ever sent away.

So, what sort of games did we play? I'll start with the most familiar games, such as baseball, basketball, and touch football. We didn't have soccer or lacrosse back then. As I mentioned earlier, most Schuylkill County towns had organized programs for baseball, but we also had little league basketball and midget football. I participated in both baseball and basketball but never made the cut for midget football.

In fact, I was quite abysmal at every sport I ever attempted. You name it, I stank at it. I tried time and time again and failed every time. The last straw was junior high basketball. I recall being very upset after being the only one cut from the list after a week of basketball tryouts. I remember telling my dad how frustrated I was at not being good at any sport, no matter how hard I tried. It probably helped that Dad wasn't into sports either. He helped coach and did whatever he could for me, but it wasn't a big deal for him like it was for the other dads. As a kid, Dad worked as a breaker boy at a colliery, separating rock from coal. He never had time for sports; he was too busy working.

He told me this: "It doesn't matter if you're good at sports or not. You like playing guitar, right?"

I replied, "Yeah, I love it."

Dad said, "Well when you're seventy or eighty, you'll still be able to play your guitar. But these jocks will be washed up by the time they're thirty-five, if not sooner. Then they'll spend the rest of their lives watching sports on TV and talking about when they played. But you'll still be playing guitar and making music if you want to."

I never forgot that advice or the fact that he was spot-on accurate. This was years before Burce Springsteen sang about "Glory Days" or the character Al Bundy from "Married with Children" bragged about his "big game" at Polk High. I find it funny how right my dad was. I'm writing this in 2023; I'm 68 years old and still play in bands on the weekends performing songs I love, including original songs I still write. I try to never dwell on my past accomplishments, but I always look forward to whatever it is I'll do next.

When we weren't playing organized sports, we often could be found playing pick-up versions of these standard games around the neighborhood with whoever might be available. But often, we would have games that were either passed down from older kids or those we'd make up ourselves.

One such game was called "wolfie". I suppose it was a modified version of hide and seek. The rules were simple. One person was "it," and everyone else went and hid. If the person who was "it" found you, he had to tag you. Once you were tagged, you had to join him in finding and tagging others. So, at the start of the game, it was one player trying to find and tag as many as a dozen hiders; however, by the time the game ended, a dozen kids would be trying to find the last player.

The game ended if the last hider was found, if he made it to home base (rarely), or if somebody's mom called them to come in. I was often among the last to be caught because I learned to blend into my surroundings and not be seen. Unfortunately, this skill has followed me into adulthood, and now it's almost impossible for me to be noticed. I can stand at a bar with money in my hands, and bartenders walk right past me and don't see me. Apparently, invisibility is my superpower.

During the day, when we were tired of traditional games and became bored, one of us would somehow come up with some sort of game on the fly. For example, there were a lot of wild apple trees in the hills along Catawissa Road. They were never picked and often fell to the ground, where they rotted. Occasionally, we might pick and eat one from the tree, but they were usually hard and sour.

We often cut a thin branch from a wild maple tree, then skin off the bark and leaves with our pocketknives. For the record, every kid had a pocketknife, which we carried everywhere, including school; however, you never let the teacher see your pocketknife, or you'd surely lose it. I always bought my dad a new pocketknife for his birthday, and he'd give me his old one. That way, I always had a nice, sharp pocketknife.

Anyway, we'd peel off the bark and have a long, thin, flexible branch about two feet in length and maybe a half inch or less in diameter. Because the wood was so fresh, it bent and flexed rather than broke. When you take a tribe of bored kids and add some flexible branches and dozens of rotting apples, you get a new pastime called "apple flinging."

The rules were simple. Stick an apple on the end of your "flinger," wind up for an overhand throw, hold tight, then let the apple fly. The results were often awesome, especially with the semi-rotten apples. They would fly far and high, and when they hit the road, they would make a tremendous splat, sending bits of apple in all directions.

Unfortunately, thanks to the warped sense of humor of my next-door neighbor and friend, Ronny, the original intent of apple flinging evolved into something beyond disgusting. Ronny passed away a few years ago, and I hadn't had the opportunity to speak to him in decades after he moved from the area and we lost touch. There's no delicate way to tell this part of the story, but I'll do my best to keep it as inoffensive as possible.

You see, as young boys, we were out of our houses from early in the morning and seldom returned home before noon. Often, we played in the woods and hills between our neighborhood and the strippins. From time to time, Mother Nature would call, and rather than walk all the way home, we would answer that call under a tree.

Depending upon how loud Mother Nature called, sometimes wiping with leaves was involved. The result was an often-substantial deposit left on the ground. One day, while apple flinging, one of the neighborhood kids heard and answered that call of nature. For some unknown and twisted reason, Ronny thought it would be funny to stick his apple flinger into the pile and then...wait for it...fling it at the rest of us.

This resulted in lots of screaming, shouting, and kid-cursing while Ronny cackled like a lunatic. Then, before we realized it, one of the other kids stuck his apple flinger into the mess and joined in. It was mayhem, similar to a troop of monkeys in a fecal-flinging frenzy in a cage. Somehow, I managed to run away before getting anything on my clothes that my mom would most definitely be upset about. I don't know how the other kids explained the stains on their clothes, and I didn't really care as I was grossed out. All I know was from that day on, nobody wanted to take care of that sort of natural business when Ronny was around, especially when he had an apple flinger in his hand.

There is also an unfortunate aspect to this twisted tale. I mistakenly told this story when my youngest son, Alex, was within earshot. Apparently, he found it quite humorous, which is to be expected of a young boy in elementary school. Unfortunately, while playing with neighborhood friends, he found a stick and a fresh pile of doggy diamonds and decided to recreate the story. After all, if it was funny in 1963, it should still be funny in the 1990s, right? Well, not really. I received an angry phone call from an irate mother, who was likely wondering what sort of psychopath encourages his son to fling feces. Oh well.

Chapter 12

This next story doesn't exactly qualify as a game, but it is certainly something that shows just how bizarre the behavior of young boys can become when they are bored and left unsupervised. This tale borders on spilling into *Lord of the Flies* territory. In fact, I took this event and used it as the basis for a horror short story called *The Hangin' Tree*. I, of course, added all sorts of fictional goodies to make the story juicier, which sent it off to a completely different conclusion with fictional characters.

Here is the real story. One very hot summer day, several of the neighborhood boys and I were hanging out on Catawissa Road when someone noticed a pile of something white at the side of the road.

"What the heck is that?" Several of us asked simultaneously. Then, the questions went into the sort of high gear that only a group of confused and excited young boys could produce. I'm not sure who might have said what, but the conversation likely went something like this.

"It looks like a big dead bird."

"Maybe a duck?"

"Ducks ain't white...are they?"

"It's too big to be no duck."

"Maybe it's one of dem dere swans?"

"There ain't no swans up in this area, neither."

"Maybe it's nuttin', but it might be somebody's old coat."

"I'm pretty sure it ain't no coat. Who the heck in town do you know who wears a white feather coat?"

"I don't know, maybe some rich old lady."

"Maybe it's a dead, rich old lady in a white feather coat."

"Nah! It ain't that neither."

"Well, if it ain't any of dem tings, what is it?"

"I tink it's a goose."

"A goose?"

"Yep, a deader than dirt goose."

"Why the heck would a dead goose be layin' around up here?"

"It probably flew here."

"Smart one, genius. Of course, it flew here. It couldn't drive here and probably didn't walk."

"Yep, that would be my guess, flew."

"But now it's dead."

"How come it's dead? I wonder what happened."

"It's dead 'cause it stopped livin'."

"Unbelievable!"

"Who knows?"

"Not me."

"Who cares?"

"Not me."

"Me neither."

"So now what?"

"Watta ya mean, now what?"

"I mean, what are we gonna do with the dead goose."

"Do? Watta ya mean, do?"

"Why do we gotta do anything?"

"I mean, it ain't every day we find something as cool as that dead goose. It's pretty awesome."

At this point in the tale, I can no longer recall how the next series of events happened or whose idea it was, but I know it wasn't mine. That's my story, and I'm sticking to it. What I do remember is that someone in our group suggested the twisted idea that we get some rope and a thick, sturdy stick and hang the goose by its neck from the bar. Then, we could have one kid holding up each end of the stick with the dead goose dangling in the middle. That way, we could walk down the hill and parade the thing around the neighborhood, scaring girls and grossing people out.

Of course, we all thought that was an outstanding idea. That's the trouble with little kids; they can't see past the immediate situation and see the consequences of their stupidity. I can't remember who actually strung the dead beast, but I strongly suspect most of us, myself included, didn't have the guts to go near the thing, dead or not. Regardless, all I know is a few minutes later, the gang of us, maybe five or six kids, were walking through our neighborhood with a dead goose dangling by its neck from a pole carried over two kids' shoulders. I suspect we might have taken turns carrying the pole, but I no longer recall.

What I do remember was getting shouted at by some adult. I suppose seeing a bunch of wild kids with a dead goose would be enough to set off any early 1960s adult. Back then, especially in a small town, adults didn't hesitate to intervene and chastise kids, whether they knew the kids or not. And kids knew not to disrespect any adult who did so. I don't think it was anybody's parent who shouted at us, or we all would have gotten a "what fer" when we got home. It might have been someone driving by in their car who decided to straighten us out.

We decided it was probably a less-than-desirable idea to conduct an unauthorized dead goose parade in the neighborhood, so we went back up Catawissa Road to an area with some trees and an outcropping of large rocks.

We untied the goose and laid it on top of one of the boulders. That was when one of our band of brothers, who will remain nameless, got the idea to cut the goose's head off. This adventure was now entering an area of strangeness none of us had ever imagined. I mean, hanging the goose from a stick and parading it around the neighborhood was pretty warped, but decapitation was on a level of bizarre way beyond my young imagination.

Whatever the case, before I had time to even process the idea, the culprit found a rock with a sharp edge and began sawing at the thing's neck. I recall my legs feeling like wet noodles, and I was sure the knot forming in my stomach would eventually come spewing out of my mouth like a volcanic eruption. But I also knew I couldn't barf in front of my friends, so I slowly backed up and looked away, forcing the bile rising in my throat to return down to the depths from whence it came.

Even though I couldn't watch the Neanderthalic surgical procedure, to this day, I can still hear the scraping of that sharp-edge stone tugging and tearing the meat of the creature's neck.

When the work was done, someone took the severed head and hung it from a low branch of the tree. Then, with bare hands, they dug a hole in the soft soil underneath the twirling head and buried the body.

From that day on, we all called that area "the hangin' tree." Every few days, we'd come back to check on the head and observe the various stages of decay and decomposition, paying close attention to the work being done by flies and other insects. It was a gross, disgusting, and morbid thing to observe, yet also fascinating for young boys. The eyeballs were the first things to go; they always are.

During one of our return trips, we saw that someone or something had dug up and made off with the goose's body. We suspected dogs or some other scavengers might have been responsible. After a week or two, very little was left of the head save for some bits of flesh and feathers clinging to the remaining skull. Eventually, the head fell to the ground into the hole where its body formerly rested, and we buried it.

That hangin' tree eventually became an unofficial burial ground for any dead animals we might find, and there always seemed to be an ample supply of such. If, for example, we found a flattened frog on the road, we'd scrape it up, bring it to the site, and bury it. Same thing with dead birds, lizards, squirrels, rabbits, you name it. It was like every week, we found another dead thing to bury. The unwritten law that summer was if we found something dead, it would wind up in the ground beneath the hangin' tree.

I'm not sure when that practice stopped, but eventually it did. I suppose we just got older and forgot about it. But I'll never forget the goose that started it all or the sound of that sharp rock scraping, scraping, scraping against the goose's neck.

Chapter 13

No matter what shenanigans we managed to get into, we never wanted our parents to find out about them. In my case, I especially didn't want my mother to find out. I was one of those boys who was very protective of his mom and would never do anything to make her sad or disappointed. Then, of course, there was the unspoken threat of horseradish. Yep. That's right. I said horseradish, a very small jar of horseradish sitting on a shelf in our refrigerator. So, you might ask, what is so threatening about horseradish? In and of itself, there is nothing special about the substance. It consists of horseradish root, water, vinegar, and salt.

So, why am I dedicating a whole segment to something unimportant? And why did the simple thought of horseradish instill fear into the very core of my young soul? You will soon see. But first, I need to explain a few things about my mom and dad.

Let's start with my dad and his free use of curse words in daily conversation. He always used these words regardless of who he spoke with, be it man, woman, child, minister, or priest; it never mattered to Dad. I should point out that those words would earn a PG rating in today's world of foul, sexually-based obscenities.

Think of my dad's language as something from a John Wayne war movie. There were no foul references to male or female private parts or sex acts, and no F-bombs were ever spoken at home; however, there were lots of "hells," "damns," and references to the various forms of excremental description, whether said excrement came from a dog, bull, or horse. He also often suggested certain individuals might have been born without the benefit of holy matrimony and, in some cases, that their mothers might be female dogs. He was not opposed to describing certain well-deserving people as, shall we say, anal orifices. All in all, Dad had quite a colorful vocabulary. Drunken sailors and longshoremen might have found his vernacular appealing.

I mention this because my mother did not use such words and didn't approve of my dad's vocabulary; however, she loved my dad and chose to ignore his cursing. When other women commented about Dad's speech, Mom would just pass off the comment with a laugh and dismissive wave of her hand and say something like, "Oh well, that's just how he is. It's no big deal."

I knew better. I could see in Mom's face that it bothered her, especially when the comments came from the women of the Ladies Aid group at our church. But she always defended my dad, even the time he told the members of the church council they were "full of shit" and could "all kiss my ass."

I think Mom was concerned about me possibly picking up some of my dad's linguistic diversity. The truth is, I would never have said anything to hurt my mom's feelings. Yet, still, she apparently worried. You see, I idolized my dad and was with him whenever possible. My dad taught me everything I know about carpentry, home improvements, caring for my family, and being a man.

I remember once I had a flimsy Asian brand slingshot I had bought (from the Gay Store, of course), and the elastic strap had come off, and I couldn't use it. I showed it to Dad, who looked at the side still attached and proceeded to repair it. I was amazed at how quickly he fixed it, and I asked him how he was able to do that.

He said, "Anything some slant-eyed Jap bastard can do, I can do better." This was such a typical response from my dad.

Another time, when I was a senior in high school, one of my teachers told our class we would be on the metric system within ten years. I came home and told Dad this. Remember, at that time, my father worked as a machinist and knew what such a major measurement transformation would entail in manufacturing.

His response was as follows: "Your teacher is an idiot. He don't know his ass from a hole in the ground. Mark my words; I'll be retired, dead, and gone, and you'll be retired, and we still won't be on no goddammed metric system. Your teacher talks like a man with a paper asshole. You have my permission to tell your teacher he's full of shit."

There are two important points of interest in that last paragraph. First, Dad was right, and my teacher was wrong. Dad had retired and has been dead and gone for over thirty years, and I'm getting ready to retire, and we're still not on the metric system. The second important point is that, permission or not, I never passed on my dad's explicit message to my teacher. For one thing, I had an aversion to getting paddled, as corporal punishment was a way of life in our school.

And yes, yours truly did receive the paddle in school on occasion. The most traumatic time I recall was when I was in, I believe, eleventh grade. We had an older, not-to-be-named teacher who seldom attended the class, which likewise shall remain unidentified. We often would spend the entire period goofing around and getting into trouble. He might show up once in a while for a few minutes to give us an assignment or a test, but most of the time, we were left alone and unsupervised. We never knew where he was, but the rumor was that he drank excessively and spent most of his day sleeping things off in the faculty lounge.

Once, when we were all particularly rambunctious, several full water pistols miraculously appeared in our classroom, and mayhem ensued. Being the dope that I was, when I found one of these pistols in my hand, I took the opportunity to approach one of the larger girls in our class with the equally largest bust size and shoot those Mt. Everest-sized rib balloons quite generously. As my awful luck would have it, our teacher must have sobered up and walked into the room as I was diving back to my desk. The girl was still screaming and wiping the water from her over-abundant crumb catchers.

The teacher asked what happened, and she cried, "Tommy shot me with a water pistol."

Oh boy. I knew I was a dead man squirming. The teacher pointed at me and told me to get up to the front of the room. I knew I would get paddled, and the last thing I wanted to do was have the class see me showing fear. He got behind me and smacked me just below the butt on the backs of my upper legs so hard I was lifted up off the ground. It was pure agony, and it took everything I had not to scream.

He said angrily, "How did you like that, smart guy?"

It seems my teacher was incorrect in calling me a smart guy. You see, a smart guy would have figured, based on his teacher's reputation and current anger, that perhaps the man might be nursing a hangover. Then, the prudent thing would be to tell the teacher I was eternally sorry for what I had done, then fall to my knees, kissing the hem of the teacher's garb and begging for mercy and forgiveness. An idiot, on the other hand, would have turned to his teacher, given him a look of disgust, made the man feel as if he was as insignificant as a fly turd, and then said, "Ha, that wasn't so bad."

Yep. You guessed it. That was my reply. My teacher didn't seem to appreciate my attempt at false bravado and decided the correct response was to paddle me again. I may be slow, but I'm not entirely idiotic. After the second paddling, which hit the exact same spot, once again lifted me off the ground, and made the first blow feel like a love tap, I decided it would be best to keep my stupid mouth shut and take my seat with the best look of contrition I could manage. If you're not really smart, you gotta be tough.

The other reason I tended to try to keep any of my indiscretions from my mom was because of the trauma brought on many years earlier by horseradish. So, once again, what does horseradish have to do with all this? You see, I think Mom was concerned that since I was so close to my dad and was learning so many things from him, I might inadvertently pick up Dad's colorful interpretation of the King's English as well. She might have tolerated such verbal indiscretions from her husband, going along to get along, but there was "no way in heck" she was about to accept it from her oldest son.

I have no idea if I had said anything, such as letting a curse slip out, to cause this concern or if Mom had just chosen to launch a preemptive strike, but one day, I found myself standing in front of an open refrigerator door in our kitchen next to my mom, and she had a real serious look on her face. For a minute, I thought maybe that child molester guy was back in town or something, and I was going to get another warning.

Mom reached into the refrigerator and took out this small bottle with the word "horseradish" on it. I noticed a glass of ice water sitting nearby on the counter. Mom took a tiny bit, no more than about a quarter of an inch, on the tip of a spoon and told me to try it. I, of course, did as I was told since I always did as I was told. My tongue immediately began to burn like it was on fire. Mom handed me the glass of water, which I guzzled in a feeble attempt to cool my flaming tongue. The feeling was worse than any cinnamon candy fireball jawbreaker I had ever eaten. My eyes watered, and I began to sweat like mad.

My tongue immediately began to burn like it was on fire.

I looked at Mom through watery eyes, in bewilderment, wondering why she had done such a horrible thing to me. She was my mom! She comforted me when I was little and fell, skinning my knee, by singing to me. She even apparently pushed my leaking brains back into my head after Jeanie saw them oozing out in our kitchen. Yet here she was, torturing me with some accursed concoction. That was when she looked at me more seriously than ever before and said, "If I ever hear you using any of those bad words your daddy uses, I'll bring you in here and make you eat a heaping spoonful of that stuff. Do you understand?"

Oh yes, I most certainly understood, and I can honestly say my mom never heard me utter a single one of those obscene linguistic morsels, never in her entire life. And to prove how effective her warning was, none of my kids have ever heard me use such language either. Although, to be honest, watching my tongue around my family is something I do out of love and respect. My mom is long gone from this world, but that memory of the horseradish incident lives on.

Chapter 14

The two grandparents I remember most were my maternal grandparents, Lucy and Robert Metzinger. Grammy, as we called Lucy, was the former Lucille Magdeburg. I was fortunate to have had her in my life until my early adulthood, and I have many fond memories of her. It wasn't until years later that I realized what a strong person she was.

Pap, on the other hand, was something of a silent mystery to us kids. He seldom spoke to me or my siblings and cousins other than to issue a rough grunt or bark at us if we were annoying him, which I suspect we often were.

We were always told that Pap had been injured in a coal mine accident at a fairly young age and had lost a leg. I'm not sure how much of that mine accident story is true, but he was most definitely missing a leg. We were also told after being rescued from his accident, his hair had turned pure white from fright. Again, this could all be family folklore, but for as long as I knew my grandfather, his hair was a bushy snow-white fringe surrounding his bald head. His son, my late Uncle Bob, had the same hairline, and it has continued on to my brother, several male cousins, and me. I suppose we could call it the Metzinger curse.

Another thing I realized looking back was that, as kids, we never gave any thought to the fact that Pap only had one leg. It was just something that was and something we accepted. Pap had one leg, but it was no big deal; life went on. As far as I can remember, he didn't have an artificial replacement leg; he just used crutches to maneuver around.

He spent most of his days sitting in a chair in a bumped-out area of my grandparent's second-floor apartment, looking out the window and smoking cigarettes.

Here is a picture of that window. But back in Pap's time, there was no air conditioner, just open windows with screens.

He seemed to smoke nonstop, lighting one from the failing embers of the previous. Every birthday and gift-giving holiday, we kids would put our names on a card attached to a wrapped carton of cigarettes. That was one of the few times I remember him cracking-wise. He'd look at the wrapped carton and growl, "I wonder what this is." Then he would grunt/chuckle to himself. With what we know about the side effects of smoking now, those gifts probably did him more harm than good.

Pap would sit in a white tee shirt and work pants for hours, staring out the window, smoking, and repeatedly humming the same tune. It wasn't an actual song, just three notes, first progressing up a scale, then down the scale, then back up the scale, then back down. First, he would go up, "Hum, hum, hum," then down, "Hum, hum,

hum." Then he'd go up again, then down again. This would go on for hours. Now, decades later, I can still repeat those same three notes exactly as Pap did back then. I imagine someday, if I end up locked away in some old folks' home with my brains turned to applesauce, I might find myself staring out a window humming Pap's three-note tune. Now, that's a scary thought.

In the evenings, Pap would take his crutches and make his way down the long two-story flight of steps and then down Centre Street to the Eagle's Social Hall, where he would hang out and drink; then, when he was ready, he'd make the long, uphill journey home. My grandparents lived on the side street at south Tenth and Centre Streets, and the Eagle's was on the corner of Ninth and Centre. Although only a block from home, it had to be quite the trek for someone with only one leg while on crutches and "half in the bag," as they say.

People called my grandfather "Lightning." I thought it was a dig at the fact he had to get around so slowly with his crutches. I later learned he had always been nicknamed Lightning long before his accident. Apparently, he had moved slowly all his life and had earned the moniker early on.

My grandmother worked full-time and still looked after my pap. I'm not sure how they managed to survive. It had to be hard, yet Gram did whatever she needed to make ends meet. If they ever had money problems, we never knew about them because their apartment was always clean and well-kept, and Gram, a pretty lady, always maintained her appearance. My grandmother had class and had great pride and respect for her profession. Nowadays, many people look down on being a waitress and consider it a temporary or pass-through job. For Gram, it was a livelihood she carried out with pride and professionalism.

I remember sitting at Gram and Pap's kitchen table, watching him drink his cup of tea with milk and sugar. The cup sat on top of a matching saucer, and as Pap stirred his tea and drank, small amounts of tea spilled onto the saucer. When finished, Pap would always set his cup on the table, lift the saucer to his lips, and drink what had spilled onto it. I remember thinking that was kind of strange, but again, I just accepted it was something he did.

I don't recall how old Pap was when he passed on, but I know there were issues with his mental faculties, and he had suffered from strokes and diabetes. I believe he died in Berks County at the Wernersville State Hospital, where he had to be placed when he became too much for my Gram to handle. As I recall, his diabetes had caused him to go blind and lose his other leg while in the hospital. I remember my older sisters crying almost hysterically after visiting Pap at the hospital, saying how pathetic and broken he looked with his missing legs and being blind and not able to even recall who they were.

My grandmother lived for quite a few years after that, but she eventually passed on as well. As a teenager, I would often stop at Gram's apartment and listen to her stories of friends and relatives. People often forget that their older relatives are walking history books with volumes of information that can either be passed on or lost forever. I enjoyed hearing Gram's tales. She also made a killer rice pudding, which I enjoyed on many visits.

My maternal grandparents had four children — Robert, Jean, Lois, and Rosemary. My mother was Lois, who married my father, George Malafarina.

My paternal grandparents were even less known to me. I mentioned my grandfather, Pietro Malafarina. He came to the U.S. from Italy with his brother when he was about nineteen years old and settled in the Ohio Valley. Eventually, he moved east, living in a small patch outside of Ashland called Homesville. He married my grandmother, the former Lydia Texter, whom I had never known since she died of cancer in her forties. Back then, the people of the area called cancer "the waste of life."

They had nine children, seven boys and two girls. The boys were Joseph, George, Lewis, Peter, Lester, Roy, and Frank. The girls were Geraldine and Pauline. They all lived in the family's homestead in Homesville. Several of my cousins still live in the area, including Homesville.

My dad was originally named Georgio Ernesto Malafarina, but he later changed it to George Thomas Malafarina. He married my mother, the former Lois Gertrude Metzinger. All these generations later, it's interesting to see how things evolve. My paternal grandfather was 100% Italian, and he married a woman of German descent. That made my dad half-Italian and half-German. He married my mother, who was of German descent, making me only 25% Italian. My first wife was of German and Irish descent, and my forever wife, the former JoAnne Krueger, was of German descent. We joke how our boys have Italian last names but don't look even a little Italian. I often say all I inherited was the name and the nose.

My grandfather Malafarina died when I was about ten or twelve years old, so my memories of him were very vague, and most of the impressions I got from him were from stories my dad told me. Like me, Dad had plenty of stories to tell. How many of them were true, and how many were fabrications? I have no idea. Either way, many were enjoyable and interesting.

One story Dad told me about my grandfather was how a traveling salesman stopped by my grandfather's house and said he wanted to put new siding on the house. In broken English, my grandfather waved his hand at the home and said, "Doa whata ever maka you happy; whata ever youa wanna do, I'ma notta gonna stoppa you."

So, as the story goes, the salesman brought in a crew and sided my grandfather's house. After the job was finished, he handed my grandfather a bill. My grandfather said, "Watta disa? Ima notta payina nuttin toa you. You say youa wanna putta da sidea ona my house. I saya go aheada ifa ita makea youa happy. Ain'ta youa happy nowa?"

Did this actually happen? I have no idea, but it was one of the many stories and legends surrounding my Italian grandfather.

Chapter 15

One such story surrounding my grandfather involved a 38-caliber revolver that my dad had when I was growing up. I mentioned how Dad often took me shooting with his .22-caliber rifle. Once, when I was about eleven or twelve, Dad brought along his .38. He wanted to make sure I knew how to use it. He showed me how to load it. Then he told me to point it at a target, aim, and squeeze the trigger.

One important factor he forgot to mention was that the gun had a tremendous kick for a scrawny little boy like me. I aimed, pulled the trigger, and landed on my butt, staring up at the sky in confusion. Note to self...build some muscle and upper body strength before attempting to shoot that gun again. For the record, I never touched that accursed hand cannon after that day.

When we got home, Dad asked me to come upstairs with him after showing me how to clean the gun properly; he had something important to show me. We went into the bedroom, and he closed the door, telling me he didn't want my brother or sisters to see or hear what he had to say to me.

Dad said, "You're old enough now to be the man of the house when I'm not home. It will be your responsibility to take care of your mom and sisters when I'm at work."

Then he showed me where he kept the 38, in the back of the top drawer of his tall dresser. He explained that he didn't keep it loaded, and he stored the bullets in a different location, across the room on a high shelf in his closet.

He explained, "If someone breaks into our house and tries to hurt your mom or sisters, you run up here, grab the gun, load it like I taught you, then go back downstairs and shoot the bastard. Don't just shoot him once, either. Keep shooting until you're out of bullets. Understand?"

I said the only thing I could say, "Yes, Dad."

"And if he tries to run and gets out on the porch, you shoot him there and have your mom help you drag him into the house. Can you do that, Tommy, to protect our family?"

Again, I said I could. The truth was, I had no idea if I could do such an unimaginable thing, but I agreed to give my dad the peace of mind he needed. Fortunately, I never had to shoot anyone, and that encounter made me even more desirous to never touch that gun again. After that day, I never even saw that gun again.

As if that incident was not enough to send me running for the hills, a few years later, Dad told me a story that connected my grandfather and one of my uncles to the gun. I can't recall the catalyst which motivated my dad to tell me his tale. All I know is I'm thankful I didn't touch the gun again, and after that day, I did my best to forget it ever existed.

I'll be honest here and say I was reluctant to tell the next part of this story for several reasons. First, I have no idea if it's even true. If it isn't, well, it's no big deal. Secondly, I don't know who all the parties involved were or the actual outcome of the situation I'll describe shortly. Third, if this story is true, then at one time, there could have been severe legal consequences for those parties involved. Now, however, the players are all dead, so I suppose all we have is half a story I can recall, which I believe is what lawyers call hearsay.

For whatever reason, when I was still a kid, my dad told me this story. He said that shortly after he and my mother were married, before my oldest sister, Louise, was born, he heard a knock on the house's front door. I don't know where they were living at that time. It might have been Homesville or perhaps Big Mine Run. He opened the door to find my grandfather Pietro standing there with something wrapped in a cloth.

Pap came inside and unwrapped the item, showing my dad the .38-caliber revolver.

He said in his broken English, "I wanna you toa keepa dis gun but hide it anna don't tella anybody youa have it."

My dad said, "What happened, Pop? Why do you want me to keep this gun?"

My grandfather said, "Ita wasa one ofa you brothers. He gotta in a fight and shotta somebody. Nobody cana find disa gun."

The next day, my dad heard rumors around the area about someone being shot the night before. Dad never told me who had been shot or if the man lived or died. He also never identified which brother of his had done the shooting. I suspected he knew both answers, but thankfully, he never told me. My grandfather probably figured that at the time, my dad was living the most normal lives of all his brothers, having a wife, a job, and renting a house. So, when my grandfather asked, my dad agreed.

He said he kept the gun hidden for many years and actually forgot about it for a while. No one ever came to question him or ask about the gun. Years later, Dad retrieved the weapon and began using it for target shooting. It was the same gun that I got to shoot, the one that knocked me on my skinny little butt. As I said, I never touched the gun again, and after hearing that tale, I never wanted to.

Years later, my dad died of lung cancer at the age of sixty-eight. When we were cleaning out his things, I remembered the .38 and asked Mom whatever happened to it. She said the only gun she found among Dad's possessions was his .22-caliber rifle. I assumed somewhere between the last time I saw the gun when I was twelve and the thirty or more years before my dad's death, the gun disappeared.

I'll never know all the details of that mysterious story or if it was even true. Either way, it has been something of a personal legend for me. I'm not sure I ever shared that story with my siblings. I may be the author in our family, but my dad had no problem spinning yarns of his own, and he could come up with some whoppers.

For example, when I was little, I had a kids' plastic army helmet I used whenever we played army. One of my dad's brothers, my Uncle Frank, was a career pilot in the Air Force and was bald. Dad had a full head of coal-black hair, which was still black the day he died. As a little kid of about five or six, I asked my dad what had happened to Uncle Frank's hair. Dad told me it was really hot one day, and Uncle Frank's plastic army helmet melted on his head, and his hair melted off. You don't want to know how long I believed that story before learning that the military didn't use plastic helmets like the one I used when playing army.

Another example was the story he told my sister Jeanie, which was also a whopper. You see, Jeanie could always be counted on to get into trouble. For example, when Dad was working under the table for a local contractor, he and his partner were finishing the top surface of a pavement they had just cemented. A group of young students were walking home from school, and my dad said to his partner, "Do you see that little blonde girl?"

His partner said, "Yes, what about her?"

Dad replied, "She's going to walk right into the cement we just smoothed out."

"How do you know that, George?"

My dad said, "Because she's my daughter."

And, of course, true to form, Jeanie walked right into the cement as my dad predicted.

Regarding my Dad's wild stories, here is one he told Jeanie one day while we were picking wild blueberries in the hills behind our house. Apparently, Jeanie kept straying off in pursuit of her own adventure. Dad told her she had better stay nearby because the woods were full of snake ferns. Then he pointed to some low-growing ferns in the area and told her they were crawling with poisonous snakes.

That did an amazing job keeping Jeanie in tow for the rest of that day's picking. What's the harm of one little white lie? Years later, when Jeanie was an adult and married, living in Hartford, Connecticut, she and her husband were looking for a condominium to buy. They found a place they loved, surrounded by a sloping hillside covered with low-growing ferns.

With a look of serious terror, Jeanie told the realtor they loved the place, but she couldn't risk living around...you guessed it...snake ferns. She reiterated the tale Dad had told her when she was young.

After the realtor and her husband had a great time laughing at this complete fabrication Jeanie had believed for her entire young life, she embarrassingly understood that her home would not be overrun with venomous serpents, and they bought the house. When she told my parents the story during a visit home, my dad had a good laugh, much to Jeanie's chagrin.

That being said, I don't put too much faith in the story my dad told me about my grandfather and the gun, but it would, and someday soon probably will, make a great plot for one of my horror short stories. Imagine a cursed gun passed from person to person, causing the user to go on a killing spree. Watch for it soon.

Chapter 16

Since I only really knew my grandmother, Lucy, well into adulthood and did not have the opportunity to be close to either of my grandfathers, I felt I should mention a man, although an uncle by marriage, who was more like a third grandfather to me. My Uncle Sam was very influential in my growing up, even though I only saw him a few times a year. He was the sort of character you didn't easily forget.

He was known to his Frackville, Pennsylvania, neighbors as Santos Blanco, an immigrant from Spain. To me, he would always be simply Uncle Sam. He was married to my father's older sister, Pauline Malafarina, and was several, if not many, years older than she was. That's all sort of foggy to me because I was a kid, and kids didn't really care about such things; at least, I didn't.

Had she been rich, folks might have considered my Aunt Pauline a bit eccentric. As far as we were concerned, Aunt Pauline was simply nuts. When I started a rock collection in fifth grade, she gave me a piece of ash-like rock she found in her backyard. She told me it was a piece of a meteorite that had landed in her yard. What did I know? I was just a dumb kid. It never occurred to me that if a meteorite had landed in her backyard, that yard, her house, and not to mention the entire town of Frackville might cease to exist. For years, that stupid piece of rock was part of my collection display case and was proudly labeled "meteorite." A friend of my dad, who was a serious rock hound, eventually saw it and set me straight; it was no more a meteorite than I was a little green man.

Aunt Pauline claimed to be a skilled seamstress and was always quick to show off her certificate from some design correspondence course she got conned into taking. She once made matching striped suit pants and jackets for me and my brother, which were hideous. They were red and black stripes. Had they been black and white, they would have looked frighteningly like those convict chain gang outfits I worried I might find myself wearing if I ever got sent to reform school.

Another time we visited Aunt Pauline and Uncle Sam, it was July and extremely hot outside. This was a time before air conditioning. When we walked into the kitchen, whose door was closed, it was more than twenty degrees hotter inside than outside. We noticed the oven light was on, and Aunt Pauline explained she was baking a cake to get the humidity out of her kitchen. That was probably the only time I lost weight eating cake. Holy sauna, Batman!

Getting back to Uncle Sam, what I always noticed about him were his full head of snow-white hair and white bushy eyebrows. Being a kid, this made me understand he was old, not uncle old but grandfather old.

Despite his advanced years, Uncle Sam was built like a bull and strong as one as well. He was short and stocky with wide shoulders and a broad back. His voice was deep and gruff, which should have frightened me since pretty much everything did back then, but for whatever reason, it never did. I suppose I could tell, as most kids can tell, that he genuinely liked me despite having no children of his own, perhaps because of that. He spoke with heavy Spanish-accented English, but after my first few visits, I had no trouble understanding him.

I was "Mr. Toe-mahs" to Uncle Sam, not Tom or Tommy or even Thomas, but always "Mr. Toe-mahs" with the emphasis on the "mahs." Being the accepting sort of kid I was, I didn't question or try to correct him. I just went along with him. In fact, I tended to wear the title like a badge of honor. How many little kids get to be called Mister anyway? Whenever Uncle Sam wanted to tell me something, he would start by saying, "I wasa tella you sumtin, Mr. Toe-mahs."

I can't recall how young I was when I first met Uncle Sam because he and Aunt Pauline had moved to Frackville from New Jersey when Uncle Sam retired from a factory job at a Chrysler plant. At least, that's what I was told. So anything I relay in these stores is exactly as was said to me.

I suppose Aunt Pauline was the motivator in getting Uncle Sam to move back to Pennsylvania. His relatives were all in Spain, so he had nothing keeping him in Jersey. As a teenager, I was told Uncle Sam's family were owners of olive groves in Spain. Whatever the reason, I'm glad they decided to move home because as I grew and became closer to my Uncle Sam, I learned many interesting stories about this man.

With little interaction from my actual grandfathers, I suppose it was only natural that I would gravitate to this bear of a man who, although old, seemed to actually enjoy my company. He was symbolic of something strong or maybe even indestructible despite his age. He wore athletic undershirts all summer. His furry white chest, back, and armpit hair were always a'plenty. As a kid, I called that undershirt style "Uncle Sam shirts." Perhaps they influenced me more than I realized because I started wearing that style of shirt as a young man and still do to this day.

I could go on about all the good times I had visiting with Uncle Sam and helping him prune his fruit trees and work his garden, about watching Frackville Community Fourth of July fireworks from his backyard, but those stories, although heartwarming, are not nearly as interesting as the stories I learned about Uncle Sam in my late teens; stories my dad waited to tell me until I was old enough to understand.

During those early visits, some of Uncle Sam's friends, also old Spanish immigrants from his days in New Jersey, would often stop by to play cards, pinochle to be precise. I would often sit and watch them play, not having any idea what they were saying in their strange language, but also not realizing they were playing for money, often lots of money.

One of the things I learned later about Uncle Sam was that during his working years, in addition to being a member of a labor union, he was heavily involved in the actions of that union. More importantly, I was told he was also engaged with several less-than-desirable bent-nose gentlemen from the New Jersey underworld.

Maybe he was, perhaps he wasn't. After reading these accounts, I know you can decide for yourself.

My dad told me a story of when he was out of work and needed a new suit for something, perhaps a wedding or funeral. Whatever the occasion, Dad didn't have the money to buy one, with being out of work and trying to support a wife and four kids. He mentioned this to Uncle Sam, who told Dad not to worry. He said they were going to take a little trip to New Jersey.

Dad said Uncle Sam took him to an abandoned-looking warehouse near a New Jersey waterfront late at night. They walked up to the place, and Uncle Sam said something in Spanish to a man guarding the door. The next thing Dad knew, they were led deep inside the warehouse. Once there, Dad saw rows and rows of racks of clothing for both men and women. The place had more suits than any store Dad had ever been in. He never asked, but Dad was sure everything in the place was hotter than a well-fired coal stove.

The man checked my dad out for size, took a suit down from the rack, and handed it to him. Uncle Sam reached into his wallet, pulled out some cash, and gave it to the man. Then Dad and Uncle Sam shook the man's hand, left, and drove home.

Another Uncle Sam story involved a card game that Uncle Sam was involved in when my dad was a teenager. Apparently, Uncle Sam was involved in a high-stakes card game that took place at a kitchen table one late summer evening. It was a warm night, and the kitchen door stood open, leaving what little breeze there was to come in through the wooden screen door. During the game, one of the losing players accused Uncle Sam of cheating and came across the kitchen table after him.

The man never reached my uncle, as Sam quickly pulled a switchblade knife from under the table and sliced the man across the bridge of his nose and cheeks. Dad said he remembered hearing the man screaming, and blood was flying in all directions. The man turned and ran right through the screen door, knocking it off its hinges. Dad said he was so upset by seeing this that he vomited. Uncle Sam acted like business as usual.

Another time, Uncle Sam was playing cards for money, and he was somewhat immobile, wearing a back brace for some physical ailment. Once again, the stakes were high: Uncle Sam was winning, and someone accused him of cheating. I suppose the guy thought since Uncle Sam was hurting with severe back trouble, he would be defenseless. So, when the man came across the table to teach Uncle Sam a lesson, he got a surprise he hadn't expected.

Although virtually immobilized by a back brace and in constant pain, Uncle Sam grabbed the guy in a bear hug, then bit into his ear, tore a large portion of it off, and spit it to the floor, Mike Tyson style. That's all I ever heard of that story. I don't know if that guy ran through a screen door like the other one or if this even happened; however, I do have to wonder why Uncle Sam always seemed to be accused of cheating.

Uncle Sam was an atheist. He hated organized religion and especially hated priests. Sam called them "cuckoo birds." Once, as a teenager, I asked him why he called priests cuckoo birds. In broken English and typical Uncle Sam fashion, he's said, "I wassa tella you, Mr. Toe-mahs. Dema no good sumonabeechina priests. Day isa just like dema, goddamina cuckoo birds. Cuckoo birds lay their eggs ina somea body else'sa nest. Datsa what dema noa good priests do."

Toward the end of his life, Uncle Sam was hospitalized several times. I don't recall what was wrong with him or what disease eventually killed him. I never asked stuff like that, even as a young man. But I do remember going to see him at the hospital once when he was in. For some reason, he had to have some invasive rectal procedure, and he was in a lot of pain.

I remember asking him how he was doing, and he said, "Ita hurts so bad. I'ma tella you, Mr. Toe-mahs. Dema goddamina homosexuals, I don't know how they can do this."

Such was the way of my Uncle Sam. Then, one day, he died, and my dad and I were both pallbearers at his funeral. It was an interesting funeral in several ways. First, with Uncle Sam being a sworn atheist, there was no church or religious service. It was sort of like the old joke about the atheist's funeral, all dressed up and no place to go.

I remember crazy Aunt Pauline taking pictures of Uncle Sam laid out in the box. I figured it was just another one of her wacky ideas, but later, I learned that she had to show proof of his death to his family in Spain. I would think a death certificate might suffice, but then again, this was Aunt Pauline.

As uniquely unusual as all that might have been, something more bizarre and unanticipated happened to me. It came when I unexpectedly met my uncle's friend, Emanuel. If I had ever met the man before, I think I might have remembered. But as far as I know, that encounter at the funeral was the first and, thankfully, the last time I ever met him.

As I stood in the funeral parlor among the other visitors, a man approached me and said in a heavy Spanish accent, "Are you Toe-mahs?" It was strange since the voice sounded almost like Uncle Sam's.

I turned to see who was there and was stopped in my tracks. I looked into the eyes of an old man, and for the first time in my life, I felt nothing, not a single drop of emotion coming from those eyes. Authors often describe criminal types as having dead eyes. Looking into the emptiness of this man's eyes, I sensed instantly that he was as dead as any living person could be.

I must mention here that I am no psychic and don't believe in ghosts or any of that sort of mumbo jumbo. However, I have always been extremely empathetic when it comes to sensing people's emotions. It's the reason I try to stay away from things like funerals. Those places are literal fonts of sorrowful emotions and often make me feel like I'm drowning in absorbed sadness.

Once, as a paper boy, I had to stop at an elderly customer's house to collect his weekly newspaper payment, and as soon as I passed through the door, a thought appeared in my head. "His wife is

114

dead," I knew it without any doubt. I felt like I might fall down for a moment, but fortunately, the feeling passed. When the man brought over his payment, he apologized for being out of sorts and said his wife passed away the previous day.

Again, it wasn't any sort of psychic event, and no ghost passed through me. There was no icy feeling creeping down my spine. It was simply that the man was devastated, and every room in his house was awash in that sorrow. For whatever reason, I picked up on that vibe.

Looking into that old man's eyes at the funeral, I felt something I had never felt before. He seemed empty, hollow, like something else, something non-human trying to pass itself off as just another innocent old man. He extended his hand to shake mine, and I remember thinking I wouldn't have been surprised to find it as cold as a grave. Against my better judgment, I shook his hand and was relieved to find it warm and a surprisingly firm grip for such an older gentleman.

"Are you Toe-mahs?" he repeated.

"Yes...yes, I am," I replied with uncertainty.

"I am Emmanuel." The man said. "Sam, he saya you a gooda boy. He lika you very much. Anything youa ever needa, you just calla Emanuel, and I make ita right."

I didn't know what to say, so I said, "Thank you." Then he walked away to join some of Uncle Sam's other Spanish friends. When he was gone, my dad approached me, apparently seeing our exchange, and asked, "What did he say to you?"

I told him what Emmanuel had said, and Dad told me, "Forget you ever saw that guy, and don't ever ask him for anything."
"Okay," I said. Then I was curious and asked, "Something's really wrong with that guy. What is he, Dad?"

Dad said, "He's someone who makes money putting people in the ground."

"You mean he...." I started to say.

"That's exactly what I mean," my dad said. "I'll tell you about it later at home."

At the cemetery, my dad and I, along with four others, unloaded Uncle Sam's casket from the hearse and carried it to the gravesite. On the way, my dad said that even though Uncle Sam was an atheist, he couldn't let them bury him without someone saying something. He then informed me that I would lead everyone in the Lord's prayer.

I protested, but, as always, I did as I was asked. Although most of my Malafarina relatives are Catholics, we were Protestants, Presbyterians, to be exact. This was likely because the Presbyterian church was located a block from our house on North Ninth Street. My Dad and I cut the grass and shoveled snow at the church, and our family attended church every Sunday. We kids went to Sunday school before church service as well. But despite those years in the church, I didn't think I was up for this job.

For a few moments, I thought I would have stage fright and freeze up, but the good thing about the Lord's prayer is after you get past the "Our Father, who art..." part of it, everyone joins in, and the pressure is off. You can stand there mumbling, and no one would be the wiser.

I remember in church when the minister and the congregation would conduct the "responsive reading." That was when the minister would read a verse from the scripture, and the congregation would respond with the next verse. This would go back and forth until the section was finished. It sounded like a bunch of people mumbling to my brother and me when we were little kids. So, when it came time to respond, George and I would look at each other, giggle, and mumble gibberish along with the congregation until Mom or Dad gave us the "death stare."

We also giggled every time the minister read a scripture verse that referred to a donkey as an "ass." We especially liked the verse, "Thou shalt not covet thy neighbor's house, thou shalt not covet thy neighbor's wife, nor his manservant, nor his maidservant, nor his ox, nor his *ass*, nor anything that is thy neighbor's." That was always good for a few chuckles, followed by a death stare or two.

Despite the biblical misbehavior of my younger years, I somehow managed to pull off the Lord's Prayer at the gravesite and even impress a few older ladies in the process. ("Oh, my, isn't he such a nice young man!") Later, on the way home from the funeral, my dad made good on his promise and told me his Emanuel story. Years earlier, one of my dad's brothers, my uncle, who shall remain unnamed, was in a very bad situation. His wife had left him for another man, and he was going crazy with a mixture of grief and anger.

He had stopped by my Uncle Sam's house to speak with my Aunt Pauline, his sister, about his troubles. He was furious and confided that he was so angry he wanted to kill his wife and her lover. My Uncle Sam apparently thought he was serious and not just blowing off steam.

Several days later, my unnamed uncle answered a knock at his front door. He opened it to find Emmanuel standing there. Emanuel said, "Sam senta me to see you. I cana make your troubles go away fora gooda. I do dema both for two thousanda each."

My unnamed uncle immediately started clarifying that he had been angry and wasn't serious about his threat. He didn't want to hire anyone to do such a thing.

Emmanuel told him that if he should change his mind, just tell Sam, and he'd return and take care of his troubles. My unnamed uncle told my dad that when he realized what Emmanuel was offering, he thought he might pass out or throw up.

So apparently, those family rumors about my Uncle Sam were more than just talk after all. Whatever the case, I will always remember Uncle Sam as a kind and caring man who always treated me respectfully and was simultaneously a bit of an enigma.

Chapter 17

One of Ashland and the Skook's most infamous characters, one who was seldom spoken about except in whispers when I was younger, was a man I mentioned earlier — Doctor Robert Spencer (1889-1969). By contrast, he was also well-loved in the community for his medical skills and generosity toward his financially less fortunate patients. Besides being a kind and compassionate physician, he was known nationwide for performing secret and discreet illegal abortions. He was also my doctor when I was a very young boy.

I remember two peculiar things about Dr. Spencer, which I never understood at a young age. The first was that my father always took me to see him; my mother never took me herself, nor did she ever go along with us. The other peculiar thing was that Dad and I never went in through the front door of Dr. Spencer's clinic, nor did we ever sit in the waiting room. We always entered through a gate at the alley, then walked down the sidewalk in his backyard and entered his laboratory area that way. That's how I remember it — more of a laboratory than a doctor's patient area. It wasn't until I was a teenager that I learned the answers to at least one of these mysteries.

The reason my mom never took me became apparent. In later years, she explained to me that no "decent woman" would want to be seen going into Dr. Spencer's office because of "what he does." By then, I knew about his infamy as an abortionist. He died at the age of 79 in 1969 when I was 14.

Although my mother might have been grateful to take advantage of Dr. Spencer's physician skill to help care for her sick children, she wouldn't want local women seeing her in "that place." The thing about small towns like Ashland was not only did everyone know everyone else, but they also knew everyone else's business. One visit to Dr. Spencer's office and the tongues would wag like the hind ends of a kennel full of puppies. That was why taking us kids for doctor visits fell upon Dad's shoulders.

So, why did we always go in through the back way at night, then through the alley and the backyard? I never did learn the answer to that question, nor did I know the logistics of why we never waited to be seen. We just walked in and sat down, and the doctor cared for me from all I could recall. Perhaps Dad called ahead. Maybe there was a waiting area in the back, but unfortunately, I can't remember.

It could be that, like my mom, Dad might have preferred not to be seen there. It was also possible that the doctor might not have wanted my dad, or any man, invading the womens' privacy in his waiting room out front. I learned later that women came from all over the country for Dr. Spencer to perform their abortions. It was rumored that some of them had been very wealthy, familiar faces from Hollywood's movie and television industries.

There is another possible reason why we went in discreetly. When I was young, say between three and six, my dad had several periods of unemployment, as did many blue-collar men in those days. We ate our share of "surplus cheese and surplus meat." Dad often found himself on the unemployment line. So, you see, it's possible that we were one of the unfortunate families Dr. Spencer had been helping by treating us cheaply or at no cost. I suppose I'll never know.

My memories of these visits are vague and foggy, just snippets of images and a few spoken words. I recall only going there at night. That was likely because we couldn't go to the office during the day. When my dad was fortunate enough to find some "under the table" work for cash, it was usually during the day. That meant we would have to wait until after he got home at night to go to the doctor. I recall the office being not quite dark but dimly lit. I remember lots of dark wooden cabinets filled with jars and bottles. Some of what I recall might be inaccurate due to my young age, discomfort at being in a doctor's office, vivid imagination, and love/hate relationship with the horror genre, which could easily have turned a simple small-town doctor's office into Frankenstein's laboratory. (It's alive! It's alive!)

However, I accurately recall one visit when I had to get a shot. Perhaps it was a routine vaccine of some sort. I seldom got shots back then because I was allergic to the new wonder drug penicillin. I've been told I had a severe reaction to the drug at the age of two and have never had it since. The cool thing about this was when most of my friends went to the doctor, or the doctor came to them (since house calls were standard), they usually got a shot of penicillin. Not me. I rarely got shots, which was quite all right with me.

But for whatever reason, during this visit to Dr. Spencer's office, I had to get a shot, and I recall I was terrified. I wasn't a big kid, and I had skinny little arms. I was sure that any needle I would receive would likely go all the way through my arm, right through the bone, and come out on the other side. By the time we reached the rear gate leading to Dr. Spencer's office, I had myself convinced that any shot I received might very well be fatal.

Dr. Spencer had an assistant named Steve Sekunda. I always called him Dr. Steve, although I learned years later Steve wasn't a doctor, just Dr. Spencer's lab assistant. As I recall, both Steve and Dr. Spencer were soft-spoken and always kind to me. I'm sure I would have remembered if they hadn't been. When it was time for my shot, I stared at my skinny little arm, waiting to feel the agony of "the dreaded needle." Dr. Spencer spoke to me softly, saying, "If you want the shot to pinch a lot less, don't watch me do it. Look somewhere else."

I don't recall if I asked where to look or if I had just picked a spot on my own, but I was looking at Dr. Spencer's aquarium across the room. I had become completely distracted, and with good reason. I couldn't believe my eyes. A small octopus, an honest-to-goodness octopus, was floating in the tank. I was fascinated by the creature bobbing lazily in the fluid. Now, decades later, I couldn't say for certain if the octopus was alive in the glass container or if it was dead and floating in a container of formaldehyde.

There's a reason I wonder about this now, which I'll discuss shortly. I also focused on the tall wooden cabinets filled with medicine bottles and jars full of golden liquid with unidentifiable things floating in them. I was too small and too far away to see what they were, but whatever they were, they managed to keep me preoccupied at that very crucial time.

The result was I never felt the shot. Dr. Spencer's advice worked so well that for the rest of my life, whether getting a shot, donating blood, having blood drawn for testing, or having an intravenous port inserted, I almost always look away. Sometimes, I have to admit I watch the needle go in to see if there is a difference in the pain level, and I believe there is, although that could be more of my imagining. Either way, whenever I face such a situation, I remember Dr. Spencer and smile. Thanks for the tip, Doc.

As things turned out, we eventually stopped going to Dr. Spencer, although I never knew why. I was probably around six years old in 1961 when we stopped going to Dr. Spencer and started going to another doctor in Girardville. In researching the good doctor for this story, he likely had retired since he died a few years later in 1969.

When I studied high school biology at the now-demolished North Schuylkill High building, we were preparing to cover a section on human reproduction. I remember that subject well, not only because it was of great interest to me and my raging teenage hormones, but because I recall how our biology teacher, Mrs. K, warned my friend Keith and I that we would be in big trouble if we laughed or giggled at any time during the lecture. What can I say? She knew us well.

One of the highlights of this section on reproduction was a collection of jars that filled a tall, dark wooden cabinet. I hadn't noticed those jars previously, and something seemed familiar to me about them. As it turned out, these jars had been donated to the school by Dr. Spencer's estate after his death. A series of these containers were passed around the classroom from one student to another. Each one held a human fetus in various stages of development. The first was very small, and the last was quite well-developed. The time frame for this would have been around 1972. Had it been today, I doubt we would have been allowed to see such a thing, as someone would certainly have been offended, raised a royal stink, and had the jars destroyed. For me, it was fascinating. Seeing these made me wonder about that old octopus again and whether it had been alive or dead.

I have to admit that during the sexual reproduction lectures, it took all I had not to laugh, joke, and whisper off-color remarks to my friend Keith; but when I held these jars of once-living human babies in my hand, all thoughts of anything funny were gone. That was a solemn moment for me. I was holding a dead human baby in my hands. I have never experienced anything like that since then, and I hope I never will again.

Images of those perfect little creatures floating in the yellowish liquid still haunt my memories, not necessarily in a bad way, but in a uniquely fascinating way. Those jars were just a small sample of the almost 100,000 reported abortions Dr. Spencer had performed during his long career.

A book about Dr. Spencer, written by Vincent Genovese, called *The Angel of Ashland: Practicing Compassion and Tempting Fate*, is available for purchase. Coincidently, Mr. Genovese was my junior high school guidance counselor. Several years ago, I met him at a book show where we sold and signed books. I should have bought his book and had it signed, but I didn't. My bad. It's funny how the roads of life weave in and out and how paths traveled intersect in the most unusual ways.

As far as Dr. Spencer goes, in the eyes of the world, he was simultaneously famous and infamous. To me, Dr. Spencer was simply a soft-spoken, small-town doctor who taught me how not to be afraid.

Chapter 18

I mentioned earlier that I played guitar. There are probably countless stories that I could tell about my almost 60 years of playing the instrument. Maybe someday I will relay these stories, maybe not. But I'll tell you a few shortly as they pertain to growin' up Skook.

First, I should state that I'm a good guitar player, not a great one, and certainly not a fantastic one. I like to think of myself as the world's "okay-est" guitar player. As a tee shirt I saw said, "I play guitar because I like it, not because I'm good at it."

That said, over the past six decades, I have proven myself good enough to play backup lead, rhythm, and bass guitar for many different bands. I still play acoustic guitar, do vocals in a local acoustic blues band regularly, and play bass two or three times a year with an electric blues band. If I wanted to play more, it would be quite easy as I can play bass and sing vocals simultaneously, which not everyone can do. But I like my music schedule just the way it is — nice and easy. It leaves me lots of time for writing, painting, cartooning, family, home, and friends.

I started playing guitar when my older sister, Jeanie, got an acoustic guitar for her birthday. That was around 1967 when every girl wanted to be a folk singer. Jeanie had a good voice and learned a few chords. She and her girlfriends would sit around the house playing guitar and singing whatever folk tune was popular then. I remember songs like "Little Boxes (Made of Ticky Tacky)" and anything by Peter, Paul and Mary.

When Jeanie tired of her guitar, I picked it up and started banging on it like I did on the piano. I remember I taught myself "Jingle Bells" on one string by ear. I suppose my dad got tired of my banging on the thing and asked one of his guitar-playing work buddies if he wanted to teach me. His name was Jim, and although he played bass guitar with local bands, he also knew how to play six-string guitar as well. Jim agreed to teach me for a dollar an hour. I said I would take lessons, not knowing anything about Jim or knowing that we would eventually become bandmates and good friends until his untimely death at much too young an age from a heart attack.

The coolest thing about getting lessons from Jim was he broke the task into two, half-hour increments. For the first half-hour, we would follow the *Alfred's Basic Guitar Method* books, which for me was like pulling teeth without the benefit of Novocain. The second half of the lesson was what I lived for. It was just jamming and learning popular tunes of the day. We did Johnny Rivers' "Secret Agent Man," The Chantays' "Pipeline," the Beatles' "Twist and Shout," and many others.

What was even cooler was sometimes Jim would have his band practicing at his house and would have me play along with them for the second half of my lesson. This time was more valuable than any lesson I ever had since then. It's one thing to be able to play guitar alone, and it's an entirely different animal to play with other musicians. When you play in a group, you learn timing, rhythm, and, most importantly, dynamics. You can always recognize a guitar player unfamiliar with dynamics; he's the guy with one volume, which is usually loud. Thanks, Jim, for teaching me about that in your Brock Street home. I'm sure the neighbors didn't appreciate it, though.

When I was about thirteen, I felt ready to move from Jeanie's rickety old folk guitar to an electric guitar and a small amplifier. When I took lessons and played along with Jim's band, he let me use one of his guitars and play through an amp. The time had come for me to trade up. Unfortunately, my parents told me we couldn't afford an electric guitar or amplifier and wouldn't be able to for a long time. So, with the disappointment I was all too familiar with in our economically depressed town, I continued to use the acoustic guitar I inherited/confiscated from my sister and dreamed of the day when I could wrap my hands around my own real electric guitar.

I was so uninformed as a young kid that I hadn't even heard of high-end guitar manufacturers like Fender or Gibson, who were the go-to manufacturers for serious musicians. Then again, owning one of those was as far removed from my reality as walking on the moon would have been. All I knew was I wanted some type of electric guitar, but it wouldn't happen any time soon. At that time, I wasn't even using real guitar pics. My dad, who was a smoker, would give me his old, used matchbooks. I would tear off the cover and fold it in half, which became my guitar pick. It gave the guitar a somewhat muffled tone and left a constant dusting of paper residue as the "pick" began to wear down, but beggars can't be choosers.

On the morning of my thirteenth birthday, I went downstairs early, before I thought everyone was awake, as was typical, and was shocked to see an odd, coffin-shaped cardboard box spread across the sofa in our middle room. Written on top of the box was, "Happy Birthday." I immediately suspected what it might be but didn't dare to hope I was right. I opened the box and saw a sight that gave me more joy than I could have imagined at a young age.

It was a bright red, black, and silver electric guitar. I couldn't believe my eyes and was so overcome with emotion I broke down in tears, which was not something I would have typically wanted anyone to see me doing. But I didn't care. I ran upstairs to my parents' bedroom, where they were awake, probably hearing me go downstairs. Once again, I burst into a fit of weeping, crying, "You said we couldn't afford an electric guitar!"

I was afraid they had foregone paying some important bill to make my birthday wish a reality, and that was something I wouldn't have wanted. Then my mom explained that they bought it with S&H Green stamps she had been saving. This made me start bawling again because I knew Mom had saved those stamps for stuff for her kitchen and had sacrificed them for me.

I loved that guitar and used it for years. At first, I carried it to my lessons in the cardboard box. Eventually, I used my savings from my paper route to buy a protective gig bag for it. I ultimately even was able to buy a small amplifier. Sadly, as the years passed, I eventually traded that guitar to buy a better one. But often over the past fifty-five years, I have wished I still had that first guitar. If so, I would proudly hang it on the wall, in a special display case, in a place of honor it deserved.

As the years passed, I honed my chops, jamming with local musicians but never playing real gigs with actual bands. I also attended every school dance featuring live bands and stood on the sidelines studying and taking mental notes. The band I learned the most from watching was a local favorite known as the Jordan Brothers. The first time I saw them, they used an electrified accordion rather than keyboards. Yet even with that most uncool instrument, they rocked the house. Eventually, this was replaced with a Hammond organ, and they were awesome. I also enjoyed local bands such as The Other Side, Hajji, Auburn, and other really incredible local bands.

The first actual working band I played in was a wedding-type band from Mahanoy City. We wore matching shirts and pants like most wedding bands did then. We played many higher-end weddings in the Hazelton area for the daughters of rich Italian gentlemen with wealth of questionable origin.

I was only fifteen then, so my dad had to schlep me to our various gigs. Sometimes, he'd drop me off at our drummer's house if the gig was far away or was going to go too late. It was our drummer's band, and his dad was the manager. After the gig, they let me crash at their house, and Dad would come for me in the morning.

Once, we were playing at a wedding in Frackville on the second floor of a social club. Dad dropped me off, saying he'd return in a few hours. As the wedding progressed into the third set, everyone in the place was lit up like a Christmas tree as the booze flowed freely, which was typical of a Skook wedding. As often happens in a situation like this, a fight broke out. It was, of course, two drunk young men fighting over a woman; however, this fight escalated to a level this young guitarist had neither seen nor expected to see. One of the drunks grabbed a glass from a table and smashed the front against the table, creating a weapon only ever seen in western movie bar fights. These two drunks were right in front of our stage when Mr. Broken Glass reached over and shoved his jagged makeshift weapon into the other's unsuspecting face. It was then I observed how badly facial cuts bleed. I backed away from the edge of the stage and sat down on my amplifier as my brain struggled with whether to make me faint, puke, or neither. Fortunately, although I felt myself swoon for a bit, I managed to keep it all together.

Some minutes later, police and an ambulance crew arrived, and the attacker was led away in handcuffs while his assailant was carted away on a gurney, leaving a trail of blood in his wake. Dad arrived in time to see the police and ambulance leaving the scene. When he saw the blood pools on the steps, he ran up to the second floor, taking the stairs two at a time. With relief, Dad noticed I was fine, just very pale. It was probably on the trip home that he told me about his witnessing Uncle Sam slicing the card player across the face; just a father and son bonding over Skook brutality.

Eventually, my guitar teacher, Jim, and I played in a local Skook band called "Isaac." I was in high school at the time. I was the rhythm guitar player because we had a fantastic lead guitarist, Dennis, who was a year younger than me. Sadly, he passed away a few years ago as well. My good friend, another Jim, played keys and flute in the band.

We played dances, bars, and local topless go-go girl clubs. That's right. Those places where women danced in cages topless with tassels and G-strings. Remember that I was only about seventeen years old at the time and looked fifteen, even though all of our promotional literature listed me as twenty-one. I also had no idea that go-go girl places existed or that I would inadvertently find myself playing one. There is a really funny story attached to this whole go-go girl thing.

Every Labor Day weekend in Ashland, we had an annual A.B.A. Parade event. A.B.A. stands for Ashland Boys Association. The parade was a homecoming celebration for everyone who moved away from town. Folks from all over the country would return home for the parade. My family was no exception. Siblings and cousins would all get together at my Aunt Jean and Uncle Alex Bovidge's house on Walnut Street to reminisce, enjoy food, and watch the parade.

As it turned out, the day before the parade, our band was scheduled to play in Shamokin at the Hotel Stanley nightclub. I had never played there before and knew nothing about the place. As I said, all my family was home for the A.B.A. Parade, so my mom, dad, two sisters, and their husbands wanted to hear our band play.

We set up all of our equipment, and the time had come to start our first set. Mom and the girls decided to take a trip to the ladies' room, which was located directly opposite the stage. While they were inside, we started our set. Unbeknownst to yours truly, a few bars into our first rocking tune, two go-go girls jumped up into dance cages on either side of the band. They were naked, save for G-strings and two strategically placed tassels that spun like nobody's business.

Remember, this was the fall of 1972; I was getting ready to start my senior year in high school. Our lead guitarist, Dennis, was only sixteen and a junior, and here we were with practically naked women spinning tassels like windmills no more than three feet away from each of us. I was in shock, but as the saying goes, "The show must go on."

Then it happened. Mom and my sisters walked out of the restroom and stopped in their tracks with their mouths agape, staring at the spectacle across from them. I didn't know how my mom felt about her oldest son playing his heart out while staring red-faced at his feet and occasionally looking anywhere but the gyrating escapee from his finest dirty dream dancing seductively next to him.

I suppose my dad calmed her down because we did finish the night's three sets without Mom charging the stage and dragging me off. My sister, Jeanie, found it all hysterical, and Louise seemed nonplussed by the display. My dad and brothers-in-law were just quietly enjoying the show. As I recall, I never suffered any repercussions from the gig, and Mom never tried to stop me from playing future shows at either the Hotel Stanley or across the street at Conn's Garden Club, which also had go-go girls.

However, if Mom had known what could have happened to me at a later gig at the Hotel Stanley, she would have never let me play again. In fact, she probably would have locked me in a box and threw the key away. Our band was on break, and my bandmate and I had gone to the men's room. As we exited the restroom, we were approached by one of the go-go girls, a pretty brunette in her early twenties. It was hard to tell her actual age since girls in this line of work tend to "mature" more quickly. I believe the expression is, "Like a saddle that has been rode hard and put away wet."

Whenever the girls took a break, they covered themselves with flimsy see-through gowns, the purpose of which made little sense to me. They were thin and transparent, meaning they offered nothing in the line of privacy or warmth. Even at seventeen, I always thought practically, and this covering was highly impractical.

We stood there involuntarily gawking with our mouths hanging open, resembling two dogs staring at a juicy steak; that is to assume the steak had two huge breasts and wore tassels and a G-string.

She said in a sexy, smokey voice, "Hey boys. I really love your band. How would you like to come upstairs after the show for a party?"

My mind went in a thousand different directions simultaneously, trying to think what to say other than, "Baa, waa, umm, dah, blah, gulp!"

I managed to ask the ridiculous question, "A party? Who all will be there?" What a dope! I might as well have asked if I should bring balloons or a present.

The question didn't seem to phase her. She smiled with false shyness and said, "Oh, just you two boys and me."
My heart jumped into my throat, and in a panic, I blurted out, "Thanks so much for the invitation, but we have to get home right away after the show. Big day tomorrow."

Yeah, that sounded lame to me, too. But it was all I could come up with. We had just studied venereal disease in biology class the previous year, and I was fairly certain anyone who danced ninety-eight percent naked and invited unsuspecting boys up to her room for a "party" might also be a walking Petri dish. Plus, I was dating someone then, and if you look up monogamous in the dictionary, you just might find my picture. That was one of many such opportunities passed on during my music career. Groupie types aren't interested in the person behind the guitar, just the fictional character they see onstage. Some guys are cool with that; I'm just not one of them.

Band personnel often change. At some point, Jim, my former guitar teacher, left the band and was replaced by a big biker-type fellow named Fred, who had recently left the Navy after his tour was up. He was a big, burly man, especially when compared to scrawny musicians like me. I remember one day being in Fred's mom's house, where he lived. I can't recall why I was there, but I do remember his mother being a sweet old woman who always called him Frederick.

While we were there, his mother said something like, "Frederick, I had a call from Mrs. Jones, and she was very unhappy with you. She said you broke her son Johnny's jaw. Is that true, Frederick? Because if it was, that wasn't a very nice thing to do."

Fred hung his head down in a posture of contrition and confessed, "Well, ah, yeah, Ma. I suppose it is. He got all mouthy with me, and I guess I lost my temper. I didn't mean to hit him so hard, but I guess I'm kind of a big guy."

"Well, Frederick, she was very upset about that."

Fred replied, "I'm sorry about that, Ma. Mrs. Jones is a nice lady. Tell her I'm sorry the next time you talk to her."

Note to self...don't get mouthy around Frederick. The entire episode was a very weird encounter, seeming more like a mother scolding her six-year-old kid. As we left, Fred whispered, "I should have broken more than his [deleted expletive] jaw."

I bring up this event because of another Fred-ism that occurred a few months later. Our band was booked to appear on a Philadelphia Channel 29 TV show. I have no idea how it was arranged, as I just sort of went with the flow. The older guys in the band took care of booking and that sort of thing. The show was called "Larry Huggins and Sons Midnight Show," but it was videotaped in the afternoon.

We were unaware until we walked into the studio that the host and all other guests were black, including boxer Jersey Joe Walcott. The other musical guests were soul performers as well. Not only were we the only white performers, but we were doing a cover of Jethro Tull's "Locomotive Breath," which is about as far from soul music as you can get.

With absolutely no idea of what we were getting ourselves into, this merry little band of coal cracker (kracker) musicians made our way from Schuylkill County to center-city Philadelphia with an open-back pickup truck full of guitars, drums, and amplifiers, looking more like the Beverly Hillbillies than the rock gods we wanted to be. The open-back feature of the truck is critical to the rest of the story. Other important points to remember are that it was 1973, I was a 130-pound skinny senior in high school, and Frederick was a very large twenty-five-year-old Navy vet who apparently had a predisposition for breaking jaws.

When we got to the Channel 29 studio, we parked in a dark, narrow alley by a door marked "Loading." Fred turned to me and said, "We'll go inside and see what's what. You stay out here and guard the equipment."

I believe I was too stunned to answer. I thought, "Me? Guard what? I'm not equipped to guard anything. In fact, I probably need someone to guard me."

Then Fred did something that, to this day, I still can't believe he did. Fred placed a loaded .22-caliber pistol in my hand and then said, "If any lowlife [deleted expletive] sticks his hand in the back of the truck, you make sure he leaves it there." Then he and the band turned and left me alone in an alley in Philadelphia with a loaded .22 pistol and orders to shoot anyone who tried to steal our equipment.

Whatever guardian angels whose job it is to protect the hopelessly moronic must have been working overtime that day, because no one bothered the truck, and yours truly neither shot anyone

133

nor shot myself in the foot nor soiled myself from fright. We did the show, packed up, and traveled back to our beloved Skook with no criminal record to report.

Chapter 19

I assume when most people familiar with Schuylkill County in the 1960s and early 70s reminisce, they don't think of the area as a hotbed for the arts. That's probably because it wasn't. It was primarily a tough, blue-collar town where most people were too busy making ends meet to worry about such "hoity-toity" non-essentials.

I, however, was fortunate enough to have a lot of exposure to music. My mother had a lovely voice and sang in the church choir. My parents listened to records by Johnny Cash, Eddie Arnold, and Harry Belafonte. My two older sisters loved listening to Gene Pitney, Bobby Vinton, Jan and Dean, and eventually the Beatles. I can still remember the first time I heard "I Saw Her Standing There." I was amazed, having never heard anything like it before.

As I said earlier, we always had a piano in our house to experiment with, and eventually, I picked up the guitar. I sang in the school chorus from fifth grade to my senior year. I got kicked out of the chorus the spring of my senior year after being picked for something called "Top 20" (ten boys and ten girls), then having to tell the music director that I had a gig with my band the night of the concert and couldn't make it. I wasn't the music teacher's favorite student during that unfortunate incident.

I also always loved to draw, especially cartoons. I would spend hours copying the cartoon styles of Charles Shultz as well as *Mad Magazine*'s Don Martin and Sergio Aragones. My mom would save me the shiny, bright white cardboard support that came with stockings she bought, which made a great, sturdy five-inch by seven-inch round-cornered sheet to draw on, which I did whenever possible.

Over the years, I studied the works of many other cartoonists from different magazines, and eventually, thanks to these many hours of study and practice, I developed my own unique style. Around 1993, I decided to give my cartooning style a name, which I appropriately called Maladjusted Cartoons.

My sisters also would go to the high school art room behind our house for summer school and often take me along with them. That was where I first met Mrs. Emma T. Irwin, the Ashland High School art teacher. The first time I met Mrs. Irwin, I was probably seven or eight, hanging out in the art room over the summer. When I think back, I can recall the sights, sounds, and, most importantly, the smells of that art room as clearly as if I were there today. I knew immediately I wanted to learn how to be an artist and spend the rest of my life creating. Unfortunately, as you will soon realize, that would not be in the cards for me.

Instead of finding me to be the nuisance I likely was, Mrs. Irwin showed me all sorts of fun and interesting things about art. One thing I recall was blow paints, where we would drop a dab of watercolor paint on a sheet of paper, then use a straw and a lot of kid-powered wind to focus and blow the drip in different directions. The results were awesome. The only problem I ran into was running low on air and seeing spots appear before my eyes. We also did actual watercolor painting, as well as painting with tempera paints. I didn't realize or appreciate how much I was being taught then.

I also got to help my sisters and their classmates build a six-foot-tall papier-mâché Tyrannosaurus rex, which I thought was the most awesome thing I had ever seen. Its teeth were made of white golf tees. I never allowed myself to be alone with the sculpture since, at my young age and with my active imagination, I was sure it would come alive and eat me.

Mrs. Irwin also started the tradition of Halloween window painting, which celebrated its sixty-first anniversary in 2023. Kids from all over the North Schuylkill School District submit images for consideration, and if chosen, they get the honor of transferring that painting to the window of a local business. These completed windows are judged, and awards are given by category and age group. I was fortunate to have been chosen several times to paint windows and won a few minor awards. Here I am with my version of "Uncle Creepy" circa 1969, which I painted on a service station window.

Mrs. Irwin also started Sketch Club, which was a special club for fledgling artists. To be chosen and accepted into Sketch Club, the candidate had to submit a work of art based on a topic provided by Sketch Club officers. I can't recall the subject of my audition or what I submitted, but it must have satisfied the judges as I was accepted and joined in tenth grade.

Another aspect of Sketch Club was a tradition that was both dreaded and admired. It was the hazing of the new members. The ritual was always the same. All new members were told to show up at the art room after dinner on a designated night. They were lined up along the metal fence at the baseball field and blindfolded. Then gallons of gunk were poured over the heads and bodies of the new recruits.

Any paints had to be tempera or water-based paints so they could be washed out of the victim's hair. But the fun didn't stop with paint. Milk, vinegar, pickle juice, whipped cream, soda, cocoa, you name it was used to coat these terrified but willing young supplicants. Then, once they were thoroughly disgusting, the recruits were marched blindfolded through town so everyone could enjoy their misery. The hazing ended with a party in Mrs. Irwin's backyard. As gross as it might sound, it was a tremendous amount of fun, and it was considered to be an honor to have auditioned, been chosen, and then been initiated into the Sketch Club. It was special and meant you were special, too.

In my senior year, I was elected president of the Sketch Club and couldn't have been prouder. Then, two things happened, which changed Sketch Club forever and ruined any pleasure I would have gotten from being president. First, Mrs. Irwin retired and was replaced by a new, young art teacher whose ideas of how Sketch Club should be run were polar opposites of mine. I don't recall her name, and although I could look it up in my yearbook, I prefer to enjoy the lack of memory.

The first change she forced upon us was that no one had to try out for Sketch Club anymore. In her opinion, "Art was for everyone," and therefore, no one could be excluded. Although I agreed with the art for everyone idea, I didn't want that to change my beloved Sketch Club; however, it did. If you signed up, you were in. It didn't matter if you were a good artist or if you didn't have a creative bone in your body. This, of course, rubbed me the wrong way. I prided myself in wanting to carry on the tradition of only the best and most talented being chosen. I had been previously cut from every sport I ever tried out for because I just wasn't good enough. I was okay with that because disappointment is something you just have to learn to live with. I felt those previous letdowns only served to make me appreciate the things I was good at. I realized it would have been wrong to have me play on the sports teams just because I signed up. I felt the same should be true of Sketch Club; however, the new teacher was part of the "everyone gets a trophy" crowd.

The other thing she eliminated was the ritual of hazing. There would be no more coating new members with gunk and parading them around town. The result was we had a diluted version of Sketch Club. I was president of essentially nothing and, as such, became president in name only. I pulled back from Sketch Club and let the new teacher run her ridiculous mockery of what I felt was once a noble organization. I did, however, have the opportunity to help do two large paintings for our senior prom in the spring, the theme of which was "Oriental Gardens." Here is a picture of me working on the paintings back in 1973 and the finished products.

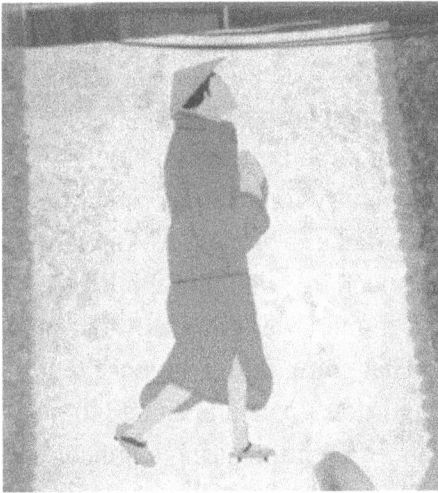

Another disappointment I encountered regarding my plans for a life in the arts involved my parents. I had decided that after graduation, I wanted to attend art school and become a commercial artist. I brought home catalogs from various art colleges to show my parents. To my shock, they informed me there was no way they would allow me to waste my time and money in art school.

In their opinion, art, music, and writing were nice creative hobbies, but they were not professions. If I wanted to be an art teacher, music teacher, or English teacher, that was one thing, but to be an artist, musician, or writer was entirely something else. My folks were Depression-era kids and told me on far too many occasions that artists starve during tough economic times. My mom wanted me to be an accountant, so I entered Penn State Schuylkill Campus in the fall to study business administration. I lasted two semesters and then dropped out because I knew I was just wasting hard-earned money on something I hated worse than just about anything I could think of.

Next, realizing I was going to become part of the workforce, they gave me advice, which I absolutely hated at the time, but since then, I have not only realized they were unfortunately right; but I have offered the same advice to many young people in their pursuit of the arts. They told me to find a good-paying job doing something I didn't completely hate to cover paying my bills and practice the arts as a sideline or hobby.

Sadly, their advice was spot on. Everyone talks about appreciating art, music, and literature, but nobody wants to pay for it. As a result, I eventually and quite accidentally found some direction and have spent the past forty-five-plus years as a CAD/CAM advanced manufacturing engineer, which has financed my way through life comfortably. I liked the profession and found I was good at it, but I never loved it the way I love the arts. That being said, I suppose that job fell into the category of "something I don't hate and can do to pay my bills." The bottom line is my advanced manufacturing engineer profession is "what I do," but it's not "what I am." What I am is a musician, a writer, a cartoonist, and an artist. Unfortunately, "what I am" has never paid the bills nor allowed me to live the lifestyle to which I have become accustomed, whereas "what I do" does.

Throughout the years, I have never ceased my love of the arts, as they are my passions. I have spent countless hours honing my crafts. An even more ironic fact is that if I didn't have my profession, I wouldn't be able to afford to enjoy my passions. I always joke that after publishing more than twenty books, writing more than 200 short stories, writing and performing music, publishing cartoons, and painting dozens of works, I couldn't rent the basement of an outhouse if I had to rely on these passions for my income.

When I retire shortly, the "what I do" will become the "what I did." Then, I will finally truly embrace the "what I am" once and for all. This was a somewhat hard but painfully accurate life lesson I learned growin' up Skook.

Chapter 20

Thomas Wolfe wrote the novel *You Can't Go Home Again*, and it was published in 1940 after his death. I had heard about the book but had never read it. I've read various takes on the title spoken by people, such as "You can never go home again," and others. I understood what that meant, but I had never experienced it firsthand. In taking a few pictures for this book, I returned to my native Schuylkill County. It was the first time I had been back in years. As I walked the streets and parks I had walked as a young boy, the title of that book popped into my mind. The idea was accurate. You can't go home again, at least not to the home you remember.

Earlier, I said that the Ashland of my childhood no longer existed. This proved to be true. Even before I moved away in 1979, much had already changed in town, making it different from the place I described in my previous stories. Gone were many of the stores, as were most of my neighborhood friends and relatives. Now, forty-five-plus years later, things have changed even more dramatically. Then again, this is to be expected and is only natural as time moves on.

When I returned home to my adopted Berks County after I visited Ashland, I decided to look up that book by Thomas Wolfe and learn about it. There is a bit of an ironic similarity between what Thomas Wolfe wrote and what I did with *Growin' Up Skook*. It was ironic because I had never read the book or known what it was about.

As it turns out, Wolfe's book is the fictional story of George Webber, a fledgling author who writes a book that frequently references his hometown of Libya Hill, which was actually Asheville, North Carolina. The book, of course, has its own plot line, and the similarity essentially ends there, but I found it curious how what I was doing — telling stories about Ashland — was similar to what the character, George Webber, did in Wolfe's book. Through the character, Wolfe wrote about Ashville, and I wrote about Ashland. Both of us are named Thomas. A bit of serendipity, I suppose.

143

As I said, so much of Ashland, and the Skook in general, had changed that many of the things I had hoped to photograph were gone or changed so drastically that there was no point in doing so. The Pines I so loved and spoke about are gone. Catawissa Road, which we played on so often as kids, now has a metal gate blocking access. I could find no sign of our hangin' tree nor any remnants of tree shacks gone to ruin. All the stores I once knew are gone, and many buildings have been raised.

I completely understand how these things occur, and I expect nothing less. One point I want to clarify — although I took the time to wax nostalgic to recall stories to write this book, I am not one to dwell in the past. I don't pine for what was and mourn what can never be again. It's fun to occasionally visit the past to understand the forces that shaped us into who we are today, but to live in the past is not something I care to do. I live for the future. I don't focus on past accomplishments or failures. I work on whatever I am presently working on, and then when it is complete, I put it aside and move on to the next challenge.

The key word here is challenge. Life is about challenging yourself, surmounting those challenges, and moving on to the next one. It's not about dwelling in the past and being sorry or angry because things have changed. Whether we like it or not, life is change, and although sometimes change can be tough, it is inevitable.

Author's Note

So, I hope you enjoyed my stories and my goofy illustrations. For many years, I had considered writing a non-fiction book filled with anecdotal tales from my childhood, some humorous, some perhaps not so much. The older I got, the more I realized I needed to document some of these stories, especially the entertaining ones; however, it was one of those things that kept getting pushed to the back burner year after year, and it was something I never got around to doing.

I'm primarily a horror fiction writer, although I've also written and illustrated cartoon books and technical publications. It seems I was always able to come up with dozens of excuses for why I was dragging my feet when it came to writing this book. I was too busy working my day job, raising a family, writing horror stories, drawing cartoons, writing and playing music, or as many other excuses as I could fabricate. The truth is, I had so many stories from my childhood rolling around in my head that I couldn't focus on which ones to use. As a result, I did nothing.

Those of you who have read any of my horror stories know that a setting I often use is the fictional town of Ashton, PA. They say writers should write what they know, and I knew the Ashland of my youth very well. In that time, before cell phones, video games, computers, the internet, and other technological marvels, my friends and I got to know the town because it was all we had to occupy our often boring summer months away from school.

I was and still am a "townie." I admit it. It is my comfort zone. Some people feel "townie" has something of a negative connotation. Not me. I wear it proudly because being a child in a small town helped make me who I am today. Although I now live in a suburban subdivision behind Wernersville, Pennsylvania, I can walk to town with little effort. So, yes, it seems I'm still a townie.

I had so many stories; it was overwhelming, and I couldn't focus on where to begin. So, there I was, using excuse after excuse not to start something I wanted to write. Although I knew it would be a challenge, I also knew I would have a great time once I began recalling and writing down my stories. Yet something was holding me back. I know now what that something was. I needed someone near and dear to me to smack me upside the head, kick me in my backside, and get me motivated. I needed someone to tell me they would be interested in reading such a book. Fortunately, I had someone who did just that.

At 4:55 on the morning of April 20, 2021, to be exact, as my wife, JoAnne, and I were getting ready for our day jobs, out of the blue, she said, "You know, you should write a non-fiction book based on all the many stories you've told me over the years about growing up in Ashland. They're fun and interesting, and I think people would like to read them. But you must make it enjoyable, like reading a John Grisham story. I think you can do that, don't you?"

I stood, momentarily stunned, uncertain how to respond. You see, JoAnne never got involved in my writing activities before. She detests horror and has no interest in knowing the kind of horrifying stuff the man who sleeps next to her every night is capable of writing. As a result, she has never read any of my stories, not a single word, which is fine with me. It allows me to write what I want without worrying about my resident angel and conscience looking over my shoulder.

But this book she was suggesting wasn't horror, and it wasn't even fiction. This was something new and potentially challenging, and she asked me to write it. In addition, it meant she most likely would read it as well. That thought scared me worse than any horror story I've ever read or written.

And what was that about John Grisham? Seriously? I could never even pretend to write like John Grisham. I believe he is one of the greatest storytellers of our generation. I would read anything he ever chose to write. But me, I'm a horror author, the bottom of the literary heap. Many callous sophisticates consider us blemishes, like pimples or a boil on the backside of literature, or maybe literary herpes.

At book signing events, I am usually given the table at the back of the hall next to the public toilets. I often have to share tables with the authors of adult erotica. Sorry, folks, but I prefer to keep my sex and violence separate. The hordes of literary snobs walk by my table with their noses high and look at me like they just stepped in something nasty left on the sidewalk. I actually expect them to lift their legs to check the bottoms of their shoes. I don't apologize for my chosen genre. I do blood and guts, monsters and mayhem, not Andy of Mayberry.

But in my heart, I knew this was a good idea, and I decided that even though I could never be a John Grisham, Mark Twain, or even James Thurber, I could be me. After all, I can never be a Stephen King, H.P. Lovecraft, or Edgar Allan Poe, yet that doesn't stop me from writing horror. Therefore, being me was about the best I could hope to be. After JoAnne's suggestion, I was blown away by the idea of writing this book and was suddenly motivated in a way I had never been before.

It would help if you understood something about mine and JoAnne's relationship. She is not just my wife of thirty-two years at the time of this writing and the love of my life, but she is my friend, my inspiration, my confidant, my everything. That's why I dedicate every book I write to her. (Which she hates, by the way.) She tolerates me and my weirdness, which is fantastic, but she motivates and encourages me without realizing it. She is brilliant and has no idea just how incredible she is.

JoAnne has listened to me drone on ad nauseam with stories about my youth growing up in Ashland during our many years together. Since JoAnne is a native of Exeter Township in Berks County, whatever she knows of Schuylkill County she has learned from my tales. She's visited the area with me on occasional day trips, which she calls my "pilgrimage to Mecca," but most of her knowledge has come from my anecdotes. This is why she suggested I put those stories on paper.

JoAnne even came up with the title. She said I should call it *Growing Up Skook*, but I dropped the "g" in growing and changed it to growin' since that is how all my friends and I spoke when we were kids. I started by writing this "Author's Notes" section to get the time and date of its inception correct and properly thank my sweetie for her inspiration. Then I started jotting down ideas in a file, just simple one or two-word reminders. Before I knew it, the book was underway. I thought with my inspiration and motivation, it would be done quickly, but in the early stages, I had no idea how challenging it would be.

These were new, uncharted waters for me; as I said, it ain't horror fiction. Since this book would be a collection of stories I recalled from my youth, it would involve real situations and real people. What if I remembered things incorrectly? When I write about Ashton, it's all fictional, and I can make up whatever I want. But Ashland is real. I decided to write the book despite my misgivings, or perhaps because of them, and hope for the best.

I returned to Schuylkill County to take pictures of whatever was still available. Then, shortly before publishing, I got inspired to add some of my cartoon illustrations to the book for your entertainment and as a bit of a tribute to James Thurber, a great storyteller, and interesting cartoonist. A television situation comedy, "My World and Welcome to It," was based on Thurber's work and unfortunately only lasted for one season.

Although this book is about my personal childhood experiences, hopefully, it stirred some similar memories for everyone. Some of my recollections were only a few lines long, while others occupied an entire chapter. I let the tales tell themselves and have no set format to follow. That's just how I roll. When necessary, some names have been changed or eliminated to protect the innocent and the guilty.

The greatest gift a reader can give an author is their time. In my opinion, time is our most precious commodity. As such, I hope you enjoyed these tidbits about *Growin' up Skook,* and as always, thank you for your precious time.

Thomas M. Malafarina December 31, 2023

Printed in the USA
CPSIA information can be obtained
at www.ICGtesting.com
CBHW080249160224
4395CB00005B/6